WORKING WORDS IN
Spelling

G. Willard Woodruff and George N. Moore

with Robert G. Forest, Richard A. Talbot, Ann R. Talbot

D

GREAT SOURCE EDUCATION GROUP

A Houghton Mifflin Company

Wilmington, Massachusetts

Contents

Lesson 1 4
Lesson 2 8
Lesson 3 12
Lesson 4 16
Lesson 5 20
Review 6 24

Lesson 7 28
Lesson 8 32
Lesson 9 36
Lesson 10 40
Lesson 11 44
Review 12 48

Lesson 13 52
Lesson 14 56
Lesson 15 60
Lesson 16 64
Lesson 17 68
Review 18 72

Lesson 19 76
Lesson 20 80
Lesson 21 84
Lesson 22 88
Lesson 23 92
Review 24 96

Lesson 25 100
Lesson 26 104
Lesson 27 108
Lesson 28 112
Lesson 29 116
Review 30 120

Lesson 31 124
Lesson 32 128
Lesson 33 132
Lesson 34 136
Lesson 35 140
Review 36 144

Spelling Dictionary 148

Yellow Pages 177

Art and design credits appear on page 192.

International Standard Book Number: 0-669-45944-5

1 2 3 4 5 6 7 8 9 10 - VHP - 04 03 02 01 00 99 98 97

Become a
SHARP speller

See the word.
- Look at the word.
- Think about the letters that spell the word.

Hear the word.
- Say the word.
- Listen to the consonant and vowel sounds.

Adopt the word.
- Close your eyes.
- See the word in your mind's eye.
- Think how it looks and sounds.

Record the word.
- Cover the word.
- Write the word.

Proofread the word.
- Correct the word.
- Touch each letter.
- Think about the word again.

1

A. Pretest and Proofreading

B. Spelling Words and Phrases

1. fade — will <u>fade</u> in the light
2. wade — to <u>wade</u> into the water
3. cape — wool <u>cape</u>
4. races — relay <u>races</u>
5. dare — if you <u>dare</u>
6. he's — if <u>he's</u> ready
7. she's — if <u>she's</u> going
8. being — <u>being</u> very unkind
9. meet — will <u>meet</u> at the game
10. seemed — <u>seemed</u> to know
11. mile — one <u>mile</u> away
12. pile — <u>pile</u> of sand
13. dive — a shallow <u>dive</u>
14. size — a different <u>size</u>
15. alike — look <u>alike</u>
16. hire — will <u>hire</u> the student

Other Word Forms

faded, fading	miles
wades, waded, wading	piles, piled, piling
capes	dives, dived, dove,
race, raced, racing	diving, diver
dares, dared, daring	sizes
be, been, am, is	alikeness
met, meeting	hired, hiring
seem, seems, seeming	

C. Visual Warm-up

Write the spelling word for each shape.

a.
b.
c.
d.
e.
f.
g.
h.
i.
j.
k.
l.
m.
n.
o.
p.

D. All in a Row Write the sixteen spelling words in alphabetical order. Then join the boxed letters and write four hidden words.

1. _ _ _ □ _

2. _ _ _ □ _

3. _ _ _ □

4. _ _ _ □

5. Hidden Word =

6. □ _ _ _

7. _ _ _ □

8. _ □ _

9. _ _ □ _

10. Hidden Word =

11. _ _ _ □

12. _ □ _ _

13. _ _ _ □

14. _ _ _ _ □

15. Hidden Word =

16. □ _ _ _ _ _

17. _ □ _ _

18. _ _ _ □

19. _ _ □ _

20. Hidden Word =

E. What Am I? Solve each word mystery with a spelling word.

1. I'm a walk in the water. __ __ __ __

2. I'm 5,280 feet. __ __ __ __

3. I'm a sleeveless coat. __ __ __ __

4. I'm a favorite of fast runners. __ __ __ __ __

5. I'm a leap into water. __ __ __ __

6. I'm a heap of things. __ __ __ __

7. I'm a 15 shirt or a 12 dress. __ __ __ __

8. I'm a challenge. __ __ __ __

Spelling Words

fade wade cape races dare he's she's
being meet seemed mile pile dive size
alike hire

F. Crossword Puzzle Solve the puzzle by using words from the spelling list. Write each word. Check your answers in the **Spelling Dictionary**.

Across

2. to dim
5. acting in a certain way
6. appeared
8. he is (contraction)

Down

1. to pay for work
3. similar
4. she is (contraction)
7. to come together

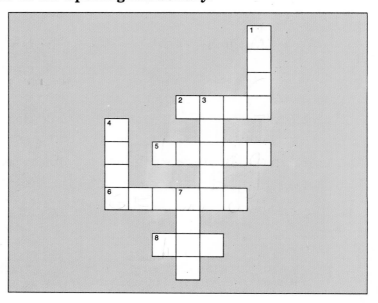

G. Finding Words The words in the spelling list appear in the beginning (A-H), middle (I-Q), or end (R-Z) of the **Spelling Dictionary**. Write each word.

Beginning A-H		Middle I-Q	End R-Z
1. _____	5. _____	9. _____	12. _____
2. _____	6. _____	10. _____	13. _____
3. _____	7. _____	11. _____	14. _____
4. _____	8. _____		15. _____
			16. _____

H. Using Other Word Forms Add an ending to each word to write an Other Word Form.

1. fade + ing = __ __ __ __ __ __

2. race + ing = __ __ __ __ __ __

3. dare + ing = __ __ __ __ __ __

4. pile + ing = __ __ __ __ __ __

5. hire + ing = __ __ __ __ __ __

6. What letter keeps disappearing?

I. Challenge Words Write the Challenge Word that completes each question.

agent	airline	aware	degrees	gazing

1. Did you ever fly on that _____ ?

2. How many _____ did the temperature drop?

3. Do you have an insurance _____ ?

4. Who is _____ at the picture?

5. Are you _____ of the problem?

J. Spelling and Writing Write each set of words in a sentence. You may use Other Word Forms. Proofread your work.

Example: he's – meet—*He's going to meet us at the park.*

1. he's – pile

2. she's – cape

3. being – dive

4. meet – races

5. seemed – fade

6. dare – wade

7. hire – mile

8. alike – size

9. agent – airline

10. aware – gazing

11. degrees – seems

2

A. Pretest and Proofreading

B. Spelling Words and Phrases

1.	woke	woke up early
2.	holes	holes in my socks
3.	won't	won't try again
4.	tore	tore the shirt
5.	wore	wore old clothes
6.	ax	sharpened the ax
7.	rack	storage rack
8.	backward	backward somersault
9.	draft	a cold draft
10.	can't	can't argue about it
11.	camel	camel in the desert
12.	madly	was running madly
13.	began	began all over
14.	mapping	mapping the city
15.	crossing	crossing the street
16.	across	across and down

Other Word Forms

wake, waking, wakes	backwards
hole	drafts
torn, tear, tears, tearing	camels
wear, wears, wearing, worn	mad, madder, maddest
axes	begin, begins, beginning
racks	map, maps, mapped
	cross, crosses, crossed

C. Visual Warm-up

Write the spelling word for each shape.

a.
b.
c.
d.
e.
f.
g.
h.
i.
j.
k.
l.
m.
n.
o.
p.

D. Missing Vowels Find the missing vowels and write the spelling words.

1. dr __ ft
2. c __ m __ l
3. m __ pp __ ng
4. w __ r __
5. b __ g __ n
6. w __ k __
7. cr __ ss __ ng
8. b __ ckw __ rd

9. h __ l __ s
10. c __ n't
11. w __ n't
12. __ cr __ ss
13. t __ r__
14. m __ dl __
15. __ x
16. r __ ck

E. Hide and Seek The spelling words can be found in the word puzzle. The words appear across and down. Write the words.

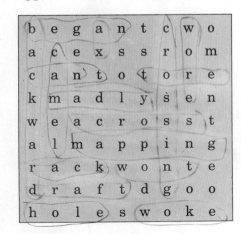

Across

1.
2.
3.
4.
5.
6.
7.
8.

9.
10.
11.

Down

12.
13.
14.
15.
16.

Spelling Words

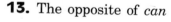

woke	holes	won't	tore	wore	ax
rack	backward	draft	can't	camel	madly
began	mapping	crossing	across		

F. Word Riddles Write the spelling word that answers each riddle.

1. Making a plan of your neighborhood
2. What the nail did to your pants
3. What clothes hang on
4. An animal that is handy in the desert
5. What you dug in the ground
6. The opposite of *forward*
7. The first thing you did this morning
8. What you used to cut a tree
9. Where you and a chicken went on the road
10. What you did when you started
11. How you worked when in a rush
12. The opposite of *will*
13. The opposite of *can*
14. A cool place you try to avoid
15. What you should be doing to all your *t*'s
16. What you did with your new sweater

G. Using Other Word Forms Write the Other Word Form that completes each series.

Base Words: map(ed) wake(ing) tear(ing) begin(ing) wear(ing)

1. wakes, woke, _____
2. tears, tore, _____
3. wears, wore, _____
4. begins, began, _____
5. maps, _____, mapping

H. Challenge Words Write the Challenge Word that fits each group of words.

slope	tomorrow	actor	fought	watermelon

1. pilot, teacher, _____
2. lemon, orange, _____
3. yesterday, today, _____
4. hill, incline, _____
5. argued, debated, _____

I. Spelling and Writing Write two or more answers to each question. Use as many Spelling Words, Other Word Forms, and Challenge Words as you can. A few words are suggested. Proofread for spelling.

> Example: How did Joan find her way back to the cabin?
> mapping won't crossing draft backward hole
>
> Joan followed the <u>map</u> <u>backwards</u>.
> Joan <u>won't</u> fall into the <u>holes</u> that she <u>crossed</u>.

1. Why did Carlos run home?
holes backward wore tore ax sloped

2. When did the animal run away?
camel madly crossed began can't fought

3. What woke Mary up last night?
woke drafts across can't rack tomorrow

3

A. Pretest and Proofreading

B. Spelling Words and Phrases

1.	sum	a <u>sum</u> of money
2.	plum	a ripe <u>plum</u>
3.	lump	<u>lump</u> of clay
4.	lung	a <u>lung</u> illness
5.	hunter	<u>hunter</u> in the woods
6.	begun	had <u>begun</u> adding
7.	lace	<u>lace</u> tablecloth
8.	fate	the <u>fate</u> of wild animals
9.	cases	<u>cases</u> of books
10.	saves	<u>saves</u> stamps
11.	didn't	<u>didn't</u> even know
12.	it's	if <u>it's</u> possible
13.	itself	the job <u>itself</u>
14.	swift	<u>swift</u> motion
15.	begin	will <u>begin</u> to wonder
16.	enter	will <u>enter</u> the race

Other Word Forms

sums, summed, summary	fates
plums	case
lumpy, lumps	save, saved, saving
lungs	swiftest, swiftly
hunt, hunts	enters, entrance
began, begins, beginning	
lace, laces, lacing, laced, lacy	

C. Visual Warm-up
Write the spelling word for each shape.

a.

b.

c.

d.

e.

f.

g.

h.

i.

j.

k.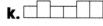

l.

m.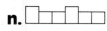

n.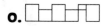

o.

p.

D. Scrambled Words Unscramble the scrambled word to find the spelling word that completes the sentence. Write the word.

1. The race is about to _____ (binge).

2. He has a small _____ (mpul) on his head.

3. Careful driving _____ (svase) lives.

4. A prune is a dried _____ (umpl).

5. _____ (t'is) time for the mail carrier to come.

6. The banker has a large _____ (ums) of money.

7. We have not _____ (unbeg) to fight.

8. Put the blankets in the cardboard _____ (asecs).

9. _____ (feat) can play foolish games with a person.

10. Kindergarten children can _____ (cale) their own shoes.

11. You must _____ (renet) from the side door.

12. The gill of a fish is similar to a _____ (ungl).

13. The door appeared to open by _____ (elfist).

14. The batter is a _____ (ftisw) runner.

15. The dogs _____ (n'tidd) bark last night.

16. The _____ (herunt) circled the woods.

E. Finding Words The words in the spelling list appear in the beginning (A-H), middle (I-Q), or end (R-Z) of the **Spelling Dictionary**. Write each word.

Beginning A-H	Middle I-Q	End R-Z
1. _____	8. _____	14. _____
2. _____	9. _____	15. _____
3. _____	10. _____	16. _____
4. _____	11. _____	
5. _____	12. _____	
6. _____	13. _____	
7. _____		

Spelling Words

sum	*plum*	*lump*	*lung*	*hunter*	*begun*
lace	*fate*	*cases*	*saves*	*didn't*	*it's*
itself	*swift*	*begin*	*enter*		

F. Lines that Rhyme Write a set of lines that rhyme. The first line in each set is done for you. Use a spelling word or an Other Word Form (p. 12) in the second line.

1. He had to jump
   Over the lump.
_____

2. She pounded the drum
_____

3. If he is late
_____

4. The boat began to drift
_____

5. The song was sung
_____

6. If she plans to win
_____

7. All kinds of faces
_____

8. We started to hum
_____

9. It was a strange case
_____

10. We stood in the center
_____

11. They all began to run
_____

12. There was a space on the shelf
_____

13. A joke or a stunt
_____

14. They entered the cave
_____

15. Write the two spelling words that had no rhyming words.

---

14 Lesson 3

G. Using Other Word Forms Write the Other Word Form that fits each group of words.

Base Words: lump(y) swift(ly) lace(ing) enter(ance) save(ing)

1. doorway, gate, hall, _____ .

2. tying, knotting, securing, _____

3. keeping, protecting, rescuing, _____

4. fast, quickly, rapidly, _____

5. not smooth, bumpy, chunky, _____

H. Challenge Words Write the Challenge Word that completes each phrase.

riddle	weather	dizzy	plumber	younger

1. either older or _____

2. either a puzzle or a _____

3. either a carpenter or a _____

4. either climate or _____

5. either clear-headed or _____

I. Spelling and Writing Write two or more answers to each question. Use as many Spelling Words, Other Word Forms, and Challenge Words as you can. A few words are suggested. Proofread for spelling using one of the Proofreading Tips from the Yellow Pages.

1. What did Will hide in his old shoe?
saved   begun   sum   cases   lace   riddle

2. Why won't the sportsman hunt wild animals?
hunter   entered   fate   didn't   begin   weather

3. When does a camel go to a watering hole?
it's   lump   swiftly   lung   itself   younger

4

A. Pretest and Proofreading

B. Spelling Words and Phrases

1. knee   bruised my knee
2. knot   untied the knot
3. knew   knew what to do
4. knows   knows the way
5. knife   the sharpest knife
6. prize   first or second prize
7. prices   high prices
8. shine   the shine of new paint
9. smile   made them smile
10. slide   long, steep slide
11. slid   slid across the ice
12. slip   will slip on the playground
13. grip   a firm grip
14. spin   to spin in the air
15. history   studied town history
16. arithmetic   a page of arithmetic

Other Word Forms

knees, kneel
knots, knotted, knotting
know, known, knowing
knives, knifing
prizes
price
shines, shined, shining, shiny, shinier

smiled, smiling
slides, sliding, slider
slips, slipped, slippery
grips, gripping
spins, spinning, spun
histories, historical
arithmetical

C. Visual Warm-up

Write the spelling word for each shape.

a.
b.
c.
d.
e.
f.
g.
h.
i.
j.
k.
l.
m.
n.
o.
p.

D. Be a Sentence Detective Complete the sentences with words from the spelling list. Write each word.

1. She once _____ how to tie a _____ .

2. She easily added the _____ of the groceries because she was good at _____ .

3. A lucky _____ of the top will win the _____ .

4. He _____ the answer now that he has read his _____ book.

5. On the playground be careful not to _____ off the _____ .

6. The butcher had a firm _____ on the sharp _____ .

7. Put a _____ on your face and a _____ on your shoes.

8. When she _____ down the tree, she skinned her _____ .

E. Sort Your Words Write each spelling word. A word may go under more than one heading.

Words with One Syllable

1. ____   **8.** ____

2. ____   **9.** ____

3. ____   **10.** ____

4. ____   **11.** ____

5. ____   **12.** ____

6. ____   **13.** ____

7. ____

Words with Two, Three, or Four Syllables

14. ____

15. ____

16. ____

Words with Silent _K_

17. ____   **20.** ____

18. ____   **21.** ____

19. ____

Spelling Words

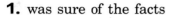

knee	knot	knew	knows	knife	prize
prices	shine	smile	slide	slid	slip
grip	spin	history	arithmetic		

F. Words and Meanings Write a spelling word for each meaning. Check your answers in the **Spelling Dictionary**.

1. was sure of the facts
2. moved easily
3. a record of past events
4. a tight hold
5. is sure of the facts
6. a fastening made with string
7. costs
8. a leg joint
9. brightness
10. to move easily
11. a sharp cutting tool
12. a happy look on a person's face
13. an award
14. to slide suddenly without control
15. adding and subtracting
16. to turn around quickly

G. Using Other Word Forms Write the Other Word Form that fits each clue.

Base Words: knee(l) history(es) knife(s) knot(ed) know(ing)

1. cutting tools

2. lean on a knee

3. understanding

4. Civil War stories

5. was tied together

H. Challenge Words Write the Challenge Word that completes each sentence.

pirate	tissue	surprised	wives	simple

1. If it's easy, it's _____ .

2. If it's thin paper, it may be _____ .

3. If they're women, they may be _____ .

4. If he's a buccaneer, he may be a _____ .

5. If I'm stunned, I might be _____ .

I. Spelling and Writing Write each set of words in a sentence. You may use Other Word Forms. Proofread your work.

1. history – grip

2. prices – prize

3. knife – knot

4. slid – knee

5. spin – shine

6. arithmetic – knows

7. smile – knew

8. slide – slip

9. simple – tissue

10. pirate – surprised

11. wives – smiled

5

A. Pretest and Proofreading

B. Spelling Words and Phrases

1. blade — the skate blade
2. blame — took all the blame
3. blaze — sudden blaze
4. brave — is brave to try
5. shake — felt the earth shake
6. stake — tied to a stake
7. skate — only one roller skate
8. scale — sang the scale
9. lend — will lend the book
10. bend — might bend the nail
11. melt — saw it melt away
12. deck — walked around the deck
13. flock — gathered the flock
14. shock — a shock from the lamp
15. blocks — cement blocks
16. pocket — jingled in my pocket

Other Word Forms

blades	lends, lending
blames, blamed, blaming	bends, bent, bending
blazes, blazing	melts, melted, melting
braver, bravest, bravely	decks
shaky, shakes, shook, shaking	flocks, flocked, flocking
stakes, staked, staking	shocks, shocked, shocking
skates, skated, skating	block, blocked, blocking
scales	pockets

C. Visual Warm-up
Write the spelling word for each shape.

a.
b.
c.
d.
e.
f.
g.
h.
i.
j.
k.
l.
m.
n.
o.
p.

D. Hide and Seek

The spelling words can be found in the word puzzle. The words appear across and down. Write the words.

Across

1.
2.
3.
4.
5.
6.
7.
8.
9.
10.

r	m	o	t	b	l	o	c	k	s
t	e	u	b	l	a	m	e	a	p
a	l	b	l	a	z	e	t	b	o
m	t	r	n	d	e	c	k	l	c
s	h	a	k	e	t	r	e	e	k
k	f	v	m	p	b	e	n	d	e
a	l	e	s	c	a	l	e	l	t
t	o	l	e	n	d	r	e	c	o
e	c	s	t	a	k	e	t	e	n
f	k	o	e	s	h	o	c	k	a

Down

11.   13.   15.
12.   14.   16.

E. Finding Words

The words in the spelling list appear in the beginning (A-H), middle (I-Q), or end (R-Z) of the **Spelling Dictionary**. Write each word.

Beginning A-H	Middle I-Q	End R-Z
1. _____	9. _____	12. _____
2. _____	10. _____	13. _____
3. _____	11. _____	14. _____
4. _____		15. _____
5. _____		16. _____
6. _____		
7. _____		
8. _____		

Spelling Words

blade	blame	blaze	brave	shake	stake	skate
scale	lend	bend	melt	deck	flock	shock
blocks	pocket					

F. Sort Your Words

1. In alphabetical order, write the eight words ending with a silent *e*.

2. What does the silent *e* do to the vowel *a* in each word?

3. Write the five words with *ck*.

4. Write the three spelling words you have not used on this page. Circle the final *lt* or *nd* in each word.

G. Using Other Word Forms Write the Other Word Form that completes each sentence.

Base Words: blame(ed) brave(ly) blaze(ing) shake(ook) skate(ing)

1. Smooth ice is perfect for ＿＿ .

2. He was ＿＿ for the mistake.

3. The fire was ＿＿ through the forest.

4. She ＿＿ held the rearing horse.

5. She ＿＿ her head no.

H. Challenge Words Write the Challenge Word that replaces each underlined word or phrase.

flames	gently	hollow	modern	watched

1. Handle with care.

2. We saw the movie.

3. The fire may be out of control.

4. That building is up-to-date.

5. The tube is not solid.

I. Spelling and Writing Use each phrase in a sentence. You may want to use the words in a different order or use Other Word Forms. Proofread for spelling using one of the Proofreading Tips from the Yellow Pages.

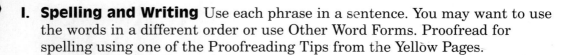

Example: a blade of grass
Each blade of grass is green.

1. a blade of grass

2. may blame us

3. home of the brave

4. a chocolate shake

5. skate across the ice

6. scale the wall

7. money to lend

8. cheese and tuna melt

9. blocks the road

10. a pocket dictionary

REVIEWING LESSONS 1-5

alike	blade	history	mile	sum
arithmetic	brave	hunter	pocket	swift
began	crossing	knee	seemed	tore
being	fate	knife	shake	woke

R E V I E W

A. Break the Code Use the code to write an Other Word Form for each spelling word. Write each word.

a	b	c	d	e	f	g	h	i	j	k	l	m
↕	↕	↕	↕	↕	↕	↕	↕	↕	↕	↕	↕	↕
z	y	x	w	v	u	t	s	r	q	p	o	n

1. hfnh

2. hvvnrmt

3. uzgvw

4. yizevib

5. srhglirx

6. dzpvw

7. yv

8. pmrevh

9. hsllp

10. xilhhvw

11. zorpvmvhh

12. hdrugob

13. klxpvgufo

14. pmvvh

15. glim

16. nrovztv

17. yvtrm

18. sfmgvw

19. zirgsnvgrxzo

20. yozwvh

■ cape	★ dive	▲ races	◆ pile	● holes
mapping	rack	ax	lump	enter
cases	saves	blaze	smile	slip
spin	bend	shine	flock	stake

B. Words in a Series Use Other Word Forms to complete each series. The shapes tell you in what column you can find the spelling word. Write each Other Word Form only once.

1. jackets, coats, ■ ____

2. heaps, loads, ◆ ____

3. leaps, jumps, ★ ____

4. running, dashing, ▲ ____

5. bars, poles, ★ ____

6. opening, pit, ● ____

7. plan, chart, ■ ____

8. tools, hatchets, ▲ ____

9. bumps, chunks, ◆ ____

10. came in, walked in, ● ____

11. kept, stored, ★ ____

12. box, crate, ■ ____

13. fell, tripped, ● ____

14. grinning, laughing, ◆ ____

15. burning, flaming, ▲ ____

16. turning, circling, ■ ____

17. curved, twisted, ★ ____

18. herds, packs, ◆ ____

19. glowing, glaring, ▲ ____

20. pegs, sticks, ● ____

■ she's	★ size	▲ he's	◆ meet	● won't
didn't	plum	prize	shock	slide
backward	melt	can't	across	lace
skate	knows	it's	grip	blame

C. Sentence Completion Write Other Word Forms or the spelling words to complete the sentences. The shapes tell you in what column you can find the spelling word. Write each word or its Other Word Form only once. If you need help, use the **Spelling Dictionary**.

1. We ● ____ be able to have a class ◆ ____ before the field trip.

2. Sometimes ▲ ____ not easy to ● ____ my sneakers.

3. We ■ ____ buy many ★ ____ at the grocery store.

4. I think ■ ____ wearing shoes that are two ★ ____ too big for her.

5. Are you sure ▲ ____ going to walk ◆ ____ the old bridge?

6. We ▲ ____ run ■ ____ without falling down.

7. I ★ ____ I can win one of the ▲ ____ at the fair.

8. We ◆ ____ the sides of the sled as we went ● ____ down the hill.

9. They couldn't go ■ ____ because the ice on the pond had ★ ____ .

10. I was ◆ ____ when my cousin ● ____ me for eating all the cookies.

■ fade	★ madly	▲ begun	◆ knew	● deck
dare	draft	lung	slid	scale
hire	camel	itself	knot	lend
wade	wore	begin	prices	blocks

D. Word Clues Write the spelling word that goes with each clue. The shape after each clue tells you in what column you can find the spelling word. Then write an Other Word Form for each spelling word. If you need help, use the **Spelling Dictionary**.

Word Clues	Spelling Words	Other Word Forms
1. a level on a ship ●	＿ ＿ ＿ ＿	＿＿
2. moved easily ◆	＿ ＿ ＿ ＿	＿＿
3. a challenge ■	＿ ＿ ＿ ＿	＿＿
4. to have had on ★	＿ ＿ ＿ ＿	＿＿
5. to start ▲	＿ ＿ ＿ ＿ ＿	＿＿
6. a flow of air ★	＿ ＿ ＿ ＿ ＿	＿＿
7. to give a loan ●	＿ ＿ ＿ ＿	＿＿
8. to pay for work ■	＿ ＿ ＿ ＿	＿＿
9. sure of the facts ◆	＿ ＿ ＿ ＿	＿＿
10. costs ◆	＿ ＿ ＿ ＿ ＿ ＿	＿＿
11. with great energy ★	＿ ＿ ＿ ＿ ＿	＿＿
12. for breathing air ▲	＿ ＿ ＿ ＿	＿＿
13. walk slowly into the water ■	＿ ＿ ＿ ＿	＿＿
14. a desert animal ★	＿ ＿ ＿ ＿ ＿	＿＿
15. a series of musical notes ●	＿ ＿ ＿ ＿ ＿	＿＿
16. rope tied together ◆	＿ ＿ ＿ ＿	＿＿
17. a pronoun ▲	＿ ＿ ＿ ＿ ＿ ＿	＿＿
18. solid objects ●	＿ ＿ ＿ ＿ ＿ ＿	＿＿
19. to dim ■	＿ ＿ ＿ ＿	＿＿
20. already started ▲	＿ ＿ ＿ ＿ ＿	＿＿

7

A. Pretest and Proofreading

B. Spelling Words and Phrases

1. drag — will <u>drag</u> it behind them
2. snap — to <u>snap</u> the pencil
3. trap — a harmless <u>trap</u>
4. scrap — <u>scrap</u> of cloth
5. bump — ran over a <u>bump</u>
6. club — <u>club</u> meeting
7. scrub — to <u>scrub</u> the floor
8. hung — <u>hung</u> in the closet
9. hungry — felt so <u>hungry</u>
10. hundred — a <u>hundred</u> or more
11. trust — honesty and <u>trust</u>
12. brush — will <u>brush</u> their teeth
13. bruise — a <u>bruise</u> on my elbow
14. stocking — in their <u>stocking</u> feet
15. unlock — to <u>unlock</u> the door
16. o'clock — almost three <u>o'clock</u>

Other Word Forms

drags, dragged, dragging	hundreds
snaps, snapped, snapping	trusts, trusted, trusting
traps, trapped, trapping	brushes, brushed,
scraps	brushing
bumps, bumped, bumping	bruises, bruised,
clubs	bruising
scrubs, scrubbed, scrubbing	stockings
hang, hangs, hanged,	unlocks, unlocked,
hanging	unlocking
hunger, hungrier, hungriest	

C. Visual Warm-up
Write the spelling word for each shape.

a.
b.
c.
d.
e.
f.
g.
h.
i.
j.
k.
l.
m.
n.
o.
p.

D. Hide and Seek
The spelling words and some Other Word Forms (p. 28) can be found in the word puzzle. The words appear across and down. Write the words.

Spelling Words

Across

1. ☐☐☐☐
2. ☐☐☐☐
3. ☐☐☐☐☐
4. ☐☐☐
5. ☐☐☐☐☐
6. ☐☐☐☐

Down

7. ☐☐☐☐☐
8. ☐☐☐☐☐☐
9. ☐☐☐☐☐
10. ☐☐☐☐
11. ☐☐☐☐☐
12. ☐☐☐☐☐
13. ☐☐☐☐☐☐
14. ☐☐☐☐
15. ☐☐☐☐
16. ☐☐☐☐☐☐

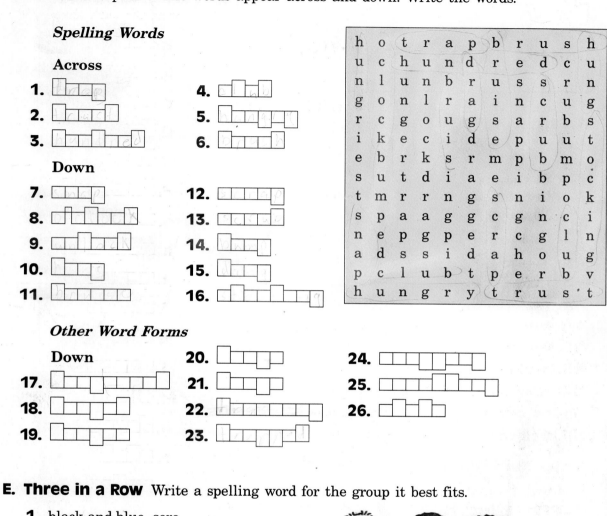

```
h  o  t  r  a  p  b  r  u  s  h
u  c  h  u  n  d  r  e  d  c  u
n  l  u  n  b  r  u  s  s  r  n
g  o  n  l  r  a  i  n  c  u  g
r  c  g  o  u  g  s  a  r  b  s
i  k  e  c  i  d  e  p  u  u  t
e  b  r  k  s  r  m  p  b  m  o
s  u  t  d  i  a  e  i  b  p  c
t  m  r  r  n  g  s  n  i  o  k
s  p  a  a  g  g  c  g  n  c  i
n  e  p  g  p  e  r  c  g  l  n
a  d  s  s  i  d  a  h  o  u  g
p  c  l  u  b  t  p  e  r  b  v
h  u  n  g  r  y  t  r  u  s  t
```

Other Word Forms

Down

17. ☐☐☐☐☐☐☐☐
18. ☐☐☐☐☐☐
19. ☐☐☐☐☐
20. ☐☐☐☐
21. ☐☐☐☐☐
22. ☐☐☐☐☐
23. ☐☐☐☐☐☐
24. ☐☐☐☐☐☐☐
25. ☐☐☐☐☐☐☐☐
26. ☐☐☐☐

E. Three in a Row
Write a spelling word for the group it best fits.

1. black-and-blue, sore, _____
2. empty, wanting food, _____
3. attached, fastened, _____
4. racket, bat, _____
5. rub, wash, _____
6. lump, swelling, _____
7. paint, sweep, _____

Spelling Words

drag	snap	trap	scrap	bump	club
scrub	hung	hungry	hundred	trust	brush
bruise	stocking	unlock	o'clock		

F. Sort Your Words Each spelling word has two or more consonants together. Write each spelling word. A word may go in more than one column.

Beginning Consonants Together		Middle Consonants Together		End Consonants Together	
1. ____	6. ____	11. ____	14. ____	16. ____	20. ____
2. ____	7. ____	12. ____	15. ____	17. ____	21. ____
3. ____	8. ____	13. ____		18. ____	22. ____
4. ____	9. ____			19. ____	
5. ____	10. ____				

23. Write the four words that fit in two columns.

24. Write the word that fits in all three columns.

G. Using Other Word Forms Write the Other Word Form that fits each series.

Base Words: scrub(ing) bruise(ing) drag(ing) snap(ing) brush(ing)

1. snaps, snapped, _____

2. drags, dragged, _____

3. scrubs, scrubbed, _____

4. brushes, brushed, _____

5. bruises, bruised, _____

H. Challenge Words Write the Challenge Word that fits each group of words.

cottage	sandal	throughout	sudden	taxes

1. income, state, local, _____

2. hasty, without warning, quick, _____

3. leather, shoe, slipper, _____

4. everywhere, all over, everyplace, _____

5. house, cabin, lodge, _____

I. Spelling and Writing Write *two* or more answers to each question. Use as many Spelling Words, Other Word Forms, and Challenge Words as you can. A few words are suggested. Proofread your work.

1. What would you do if your new shoes hurt your feet?

snap – sandal – hung – hundred – stocking

Example: *I would hang the sandals in my closet and never wear*

them again.

2. What would you do if your parents owned a beautiful summer home?

throughout – club – hungry – brush – cottage

3. What would you tell your friend if you damaged her new bicycle?

drag – bump – scrub – o'clock – sudden

8

A. Pretest and Proofreading

B. Spelling Words and Phrases

1.	trim	a beard to <u>trim</u>
2.	whip	crack of the <u>whip</u>
3.	quit	will never <u>quit</u>
4.	quite	not <u>quite</u> ready
5.	tribe	peaceful <u>tribe</u>
6.	pride	full of <u>pride</u>
7.	crime	solved the <u>crime</u>
8.	strike	to <u>strike</u> out
9.	kept	<u>kept</u> apart
10.	slept	<u>slept</u> soundly
11.	fresh	<u>fresh</u> fish for sale
12.	check	cashed a <u>check</u>
13.	shell	<u>shell</u> on the beach
14.	spend	to <u>spend</u> money
15.	press	printing <u>press</u>
16.	yellow	<u>yellow</u> ribbon

Other Word Forms

trims, trimmed, trimming	sleep, sleeps, sleeping, sleepy, sleepier, sleepiest
whips, whipped, whipping	freshly, fresher, freshest
quits, quitting, quitter	checks, checked, checking
tribes, tribal	shells, shelled, shelling
prides, prideful	spends, spending, spent, spender
crimes, criminal	presses, pressed, pressing
strikes, striking, struck	yellows, yellowed
keep, keeps, keeping, keeper	

C. Visual Warm-up

Write the spelling word for each shape.

a.

b.

c.

d.

e.

f.

g.

h.

i.

j.

k.

l.

m.

n.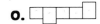

o.

p.

D. Missing Vowels Find the missing vowels and write the spelling words.

1. pr __ d __
2. q __ __ t __
3. k __ pt
4. sh __ ll
5. y __ ll __ w
6. tr __ m
7. fr __ sh
8. pr __ ss
9. wh __ p
10. cr __ m __
11. q __ __ t
12. ch __ ck
13. sp __ nd
14. tr __ b __
15. sl __ pt
16. str __ k __

E. Scrambled Words Unscramble the scrambled word to find the spelling word that completes the sentence. Write the word.

1. We will _____ (tuiq) working at five.
2. Buy some _____ (shefr) milk for dinner.
3. Don't _____ (ndesp) too much time in the sun.
4. She _____ (ptsle) comfortably on the couch.
5. Don't try to _____ (ikestr) the baseball too hard.
6. The _____ (meicr) was committed at midnight.
7. Use these clippers to _____ (mitr) the hedge.
8. Some animal once lived in this _____ (lelsh).
9. _____ (sespr) the strips of wood together.
10. He learned the language of the _____ (ebitr).
11. She has always _____ (ptek) this lucky coin.
12. We were _____ (teqiu) pleased to hear the good news.
13. Use blue paint and _____ (lleyow) paint to make green.
14. Write your name on the _____ (eckch).
15. _____ (dipre) is the result of a job well done.
16. Use this spoon to _____ (piwh) the cake batter.

Spelling Words

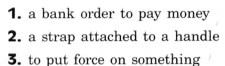

trim	whip	quit	quite	tribe	pride	crime
strike	kept	slept	fresh	check	shell	spend
press	yellow					

F. Words and Meanings Write a spelling word for each meaning. Check your answers in the **Spelling Dictionary**.

1. a bank order to pay money
2. a strap attached to a handle
3. to put force on something
4. to make neat by cutting
5. to give up
6. an unlawful action
7. to hit
8. rested
9. had for a long time
10. to pay out money
11. just made
12. a group of people
13. a hard covering on some animals
14. pleasure in one's actions
15. a color
16. completely

G. Using Other Word Forms Write the Other Word Form that completes each sentence.

Base Words: trim(ing) quit(er) crime(al) strike(uck) sleep(ing)

1. I keep trying so that I won't be called a ____ .

2. He was ____ very peacefully.

3. My mother is ____ my hair.

4. The police officer led the ____ to the jail.

5. The batter ____ out.

H. Challenge Words Write the Challenge Word that completes each sentence.

dial	seventy	high school	shelves	widow

1. Once we turned a knob; now we turn a ____ .

2. Once we stored them in boxes; now we store them on ____ .

3. Once she was married; now she's a ____ .

4. Once there were sixty; now there are ____ .

5. Once they were in ____ ; now they're in college.

I. Spelling and Writing Use each phrase in a sentence. You may want to use the words in a different order or use Other Word Forms. Proofread for spelling using one of the Proofreading Tips from the Yellow Pages.

1. can <u>trim</u> the sails

2. <u>whip</u> the cream

3. time to <u>quit</u>

4. <u>quite</u> a few ideas

5. chief of the <u>tribe</u>

6. a <u>pride</u> of lions

7. is fighting <u>crime</u>

8. workers on <u>strike</u>

9. <u>kept</u> his word

10. <u>slept</u> on the couch

11. <u>fresh</u> water

12. paid the <u>check</u>

13. <u>shell</u> the walnuts

14. <u>spend</u> your time

15. <u>press</u> the grapes

16. <u>yellow</u> with age

9

A. Pretest and Proofreading

B. Spelling Words and Phrases

1.	sail	lowered the sail
2.	jail	was put in jail
3.	nails	hammered the nails
4.	wait	if you wait
5.	pain	pain in my neck
6.	again	phoned once again
7.	swim	learned to swim
8.	thick	thick and thin
9.	brick	the brick wall
10.	trick	a magic trick
11.	drill	the sound of the drill
12.	skill	learned a new skill
13.	loud	a long, loud cheer
14.	proud	felt very proud
15.	shout	a shout of joy
16.	outfits	new camping outfits

Other Word Forms

sails, sailed, sailing, sailor
jails, jailed, jailer
nail, nailed, nailing
waits, waited, waiting, waiter
pains, painful
swims, swam, swimming
thicker, thickest, thickly
bricks
tricks, tricky, trickier, trickiest
drills, drilled, drilling
skills, skillful, skillfully, skilled
louder, loudest, loudly
proudly, prouder, proudest
shouts, shouted, shouting
outfit, outfitted, outfitting

C. Visual Warm-up
Write the spelling word for each shape.

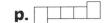

a.

b.

c.

d.

e.

f.

g.

h.

i.

j.

k.

l.

m.

n.

o.

p.

D. Sort Your Words

1. Write the spelling words in groups that rhyme.

a. ____

b. ____

c. ____

d. ____

e. ____

f. ____

g. ____

h. ____

i. ____

2. Write the seven spelling words that did not fit into a rhyming group. Put a check beside the compound word.

E. Word Search
The spelling words can be found in the word puzzle. The words appear across and down. Write the words.

Across

1.
2.
3.
4.
5.
6.
7.
8.

s	a	i	l	b	p	a	i	n
h	e	s	p	r	o	u	d	o
o	u	t	f	i	t	s	w	e
u	n	r	o	c	d	k	a	t
t	h	i	c	k	r	i	i	s
a	l	c	m	s	i	l	t	s
g	o	k	s	w	l	l	m	n
a	s	j	a	i	l	o	u	d
i	n	t	o	m	e	t	s	y
n	a	i	l	s	t	p	o	e

Down

9.
10.
11.
12.
13.
14.
15.
16.

Spelling Words

sail	jail	nails	wait	pain	again	swim
thick	brick	trick	drill	skill	loud	proud
shout	outfits					

F. Words and Meanings Write a spelling word for each meaning. Check your answers in the **Spelling Dictionary**.

1. pointed metal pieces that hold things together
2. material that catches wind on a boat
3. to move in water with arms and legs
4. a place where lawbreakers are kept
5. the ability to do something well
6. a tool for making holes
7. a block of baked clay
8. feeling very pleased
9. to stay in a place
10. sets of equipment
11. one more time
12. a clever act
13. a loud cry
14. not quiet
15. not thin
16. hurt

G. Using Other Word Forms Write the Other Word Form that fits each clue.

Base Words: sail(or) tricky(er) swim(ing) outfit(ed) pain(ful)

1. more clever

2. doing laps in a pool

3. describes a broken leg

4. naval person

5. dressed up

H. Challenge Words Write the Challenge Word to complete the short story.

amazement	waited	finished	downtown	railroad

On our way **(1.)** _____ we crossed over the **(2.)** _____

tracks. To our **(3.)** _____ , we heard a loud, strange whistle.

When the sound **(4.)** _____ , we **(5.)** _____ to see the

train that made such an eerie sound. No train came, however.

I. Spelling and Writing Write two or more questions about each statement.
Use as many Spelling Words, Other Word Forms, and Challenge Words as you
can. A few words are suggested. Proofread for spelling using one of the
Proofreading Tips from the Yellow Pages.

> Example: It was exciting to watch the construction of a new building.
>   nails   skill   shout   loud   drill   brick
>
> Did you hear the workers <u>shout</u> <u>loudly</u> for <u>bricks</u> and cement?
> Did it take much <u>skill</u> to use a <u>nail</u> gun?

1. Building a ship model takes a lot of patience.
  sail   wait   thick   tricky   nails   finished

2. Visiting a new city is interesting.
  outfits   brick   jail   shouting   drill   swim   railroad

3. Jumping rope can be good exercise.
  painful   skill   loud   proud   again   amazement

10

A. Pretest and Proofreading

B. Spelling Words and Phrases

1.	chase	a dangerous <u>chase</u>
2.	space	far into <u>space</u>
3.	trace	a <u>trace</u> of smoke
4.	scrape	to <u>scrape</u> the plate
5.	frame	the picture <u>frame</u>
6.	shame	a <u>shame</u> to miss the parade
7.	share	a <u>share</u> of the dessert
8.	gown	white wedding <u>gown</u>
9.	clown	a <u>clown</u> with big feet
10.	power	<u>power</u> tools
11.	tower	tall steel <u>tower</u>
12.	shower	cold <u>shower</u>
13.	crowd	a <u>crowd</u> at the game
14.	homesick	<u>homesick</u> camper
15.	notebooks	<u>notebooks</u> for school
16.	sore	<u>sore</u> toe

Other Word Forms

chases, chased, chasing
spaces, spaced, spacing
traces, traced, tracing
scrapes, scraped, scraping
frames
shames, shameful,
  shamed, shaming
shares, shared, sharing
gowns

clowns, clowned
powers, powerful
towers, towered, towering
showers, showered,
  showering
crowds, crowded
homesickness
notebook
sorely, sorer, sorest

C. Visual Warm-up

Write the spelling
word for each shape.

a.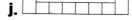

b.

c.

d.

e.

f.

g.

h.

i.

j.

k.

l.

m.

n.

o.

p.

D. Finding Words The words in the spelling list appear in the beginning (A-H), middle (I-Q), or end (R-Z) of the **Spelling Dictionary**. Write each word.

Beginning A-H		Middle I-Q		End R-Z	
1. ____	4. ____	7. ____	8. ____	9. ____	13. ____
2. ____	5. ____			10. ____	14. ____
3. ____	6. ____			11. ____	15. ____
				12. ____	16. ____

E. Sort Your Words Write each spelling word. Beside each word write an Other Word Form (p. 40).

Words with *ow*	Other Word Form	Words with a Long *a*	Other Word Form
1. ____	____	10. ____	____
2. ____	____	11. ____	____
3. ____	____	12. ____	____
4. ____	____	13. ____	____
5. ____	____	14. ____	____
6. ____	____	15. ____	____

Words with *sh*	Other Word Form	Words with a Long *o*	Other Word Form
7. ____	____	16. ____	____
8. ____	____	17. ____	____
9. ____	____		

18. Write the two words that fit under more than one heading.

19. Write the word that does not fit any heading.

Spelling Words

chase	space	trace	scrape	frame	shame
share	gown	clown	power	tower	shower
crowd	homesick	notebooks	sore		

F. Name the Book Write a spelling word for each clue. Then join the boxed letters and write the title of a famous storybook.

1. what a _____   _ _ _ ☐ _

2. painful   _ ☐ _ _

3. to draw over   ☐ _ _ _ _

4. to divide into parts   _ ☐ _ _ _

5. rain   _ _ _ _ ☐ _

6. a picture _____   _ ☐ _ _

7. dress   ☐ _ _ _

8. lots of people   _ _ ☐ _

9. a tall, slender building   _ ☐ _ _ _

10. to rub off   ☐ _ _ _ _ _

11. to run after   _ _ _ _ ☐

12. school supplies   _ _ ☐ _ _ _ _ _

13. an open area   _ _ ☐ _ _

14. a joker   _ ☐ _ _ _

15. strength   _ _ _ ☐ _

16. missing one's home   _ _ _ _ ☐ _ _ _

17. Write the name of the famous storybook.

G. Using Other Word Forms
Add an ending to each word to write an Other Word Form.

1. chase + ing = _____

2. space + ing = _____

3. trace + ing = _____

4. scrape + ing = _____

5. share + ing = _____

6. What letter keeps disappearing? _____

H. Challenge Words
Write the Challenge Word that completes each sentence.

chores	compared	coward	enclosed	frowned

1. The payment is _____ in the envelope.

2. The children finished their _____ .

3. Do you expect a _____ to be the hero?

4. The clown both smiled and _____ throughout his act.

5. _____ to yesterday, it's hot today.

I. Spelling and Writing
Write each set of words in a sentence. You may use Other Word Forms. Proofread your work.

1. homesick – crowd

2. scrape – sore

3. shower – power

4. tower – space

5. frame – share

6. shame – clown

7. notebooks – trace

8. chase – gown

9. chores – compared

10. coward – frowned

11. enclosed – notebook

11

A. Pretest and Proofreading

B. Spelling Words and Phrases

1.	mild	mild weather
2.	bind	to bind the book
3.	blind	a blind corner
4.	climb	whenever they climb
5.	higher	the higher of the two flags
6.	highest	the highest mountain
7.	highway	the longest highway
8.	mighty	a mighty roar
9.	post	fence post
10.	mostly	mostly in the morning
11.	almost	almost there
12.	sort	some sort of game
13.	sword	a dull, broad sword
14.	worn	worn only in winter
15.	worth	our money's worth
16.	worry	nothing to worry about

Other Word Forms

milder, mildest, mildly
binds, binder, binding,
   bound
blinds, blinded, blinding,
   blindly
climbs, climbed, climbing
high, highly
highways
might, mightier, mightiest

posts, posted, posting
much, more, most
sorts, sorted, sorting
swords
wear, wore, wearing
worthless, worthy
worries, worried,
   worrying

C. Visual Warm-up
Write the spelling word for each shape.

a.
b.
c.
d.
e.
f.
g.
h.
i.
j.
k.
l.
m.
n.
o.
p.

D. All in a Row Write the sixteen spelling words in alphabetical order. Then join the boxed letters and write four hidden words.

1. _ _ ☐ _ _ _

2. _ ☐ _ _

3. _ ☐ _ _ _

4. _ ☐ _ _ _

5. Hidden Word =

6. _ _ _ ☐ _ _

7. _ ☐ _ _ _ _ _

8. _ _ ☐ _ _ _

9. _ _ _ ☐ _ _

10. Hidden Word =

11. _ _ _ ☐ _ _

12. _ ☐ _ _ _ _

13. _ _ ☐ _

14. _ _ _ ☐

15. Hidden Word =

16. _ _ _ _ ☐

17. _ ☐ _ _

18. _ ☐ _ _ _

19. _ _ ☐ _ _

20. Hidden Word =

E. Base Words The spelling list contains eleven base words and five words that are not base words. Write each spelling word.

Words That Are Not Base Words	Base Words	Words That Are Not Base Words	Base Words
1. worthy	_____	9. blindly	_____
2. worrying	_____	10. sorting	_____
3. highways	_____	11. _____	high
4. mildly	_____	12. _____	high
5. swords	_____	13. _____	might
6. posted	_____	14. _____	wear
7. binder	_____	15. _____	much
8. climbing	_____		

16. Write the one base word not used above.

Spelling Words

mild	bind	blind	climb	higher	highest
highway	mighty	post	mostly	almost	sort
sword	worn	worth	worry		

F. Three in a Row Write a spelling word for the group it best fits.

1. feel troubled, be uneasy, _____
2. hidden, not seeing, _____
3. nearly, close to, _____
4. not hot, not cold, _____
5. value, importance, _____
6. kind, type, _____
7. ragged, damaged, _____
8. tie together, glue, _____
9. wood marker, fence, holder, _____
10. mainly, for the most part, _____

G. Using Other Word Forms Write the Other Word Form that completes each phrase.

Base Words: bind(ing) mighty(er) worth(less) climb(ing) mild(ly)

1. not strongly, but ____

2. not valuable, but ____

3. not untying, but ____

4. not falling, but ____

5. not weaker, but ____

H. Challenge Words Write the Challenge Word that fits each group of words.

cords	blindfold	bride	throat	scarecrow

1. marry, vows, groom, ____

2. handkerchief, eyes, cover, ____

3. knotted, strings, ropes, ____

4. frighten, birds, cornfield, ____

5. voice box, swallow, choke, ____

I. Spelling and Writing Write two or more questions about each statement. Use as many Spelling Words, Other Word Forms, and Challenge Words as you can. A few words are suggested. Proofread for spelling using one of the Proofreading Tips from the Yellow Pages.

1. The flowing river flooded the land.
post   mighty   highway   climbed   almost   highest

Example: Did you know that the water <u>almost</u> <u>climbed</u> to the level
of the <u>highway</u>?

2. A field trip to a museum can be exciting.
worn   sword   mostly   sorted   higher   worth   bride

3. The hot sun was a problem for the hikers.
mild   bind   blind   climbing   worry   throat

REVIEWING LESSONS 7-11

bruise	hung	outfits	proud	thick
crime	hungry	pain	quit	unlock
higher	kept	power	shame	worry
homesick	mighty	pride	sore	worth

A. Hide and Seek Twenty Other Word Forms can be found in the word puzzle. The words appear across and down. Write each word. If you need help, use the **Spelling Dictionary**.

Across

1.
2.
3.
4.
5.
6.
7.
8.
9.

```
t h i c k e r b s h a m e d q
h u n g r i e r x s o r e l y
a m p a i n f u l n e u t z s
n c f k l r q i n h g n p v w
g k e e p t u s o a b l e h o
w i z a o r i e p p o o s l r
h b c d w f t d r r i c p a r
c t h g e s s u i o r k c d i
r w j o r e f w d u b e h o e
i o u t f i t z e d o d i t d
m r v n u l d o s l y v g r e
i t a b l c h k p y s c h w a
n h z h o m e s i c k n e s s
a y e r u k n t b m o v s i r
l m i g h t i e r u e j t l n
```

Down

10.
11.
12.
13.
14.
15.
16.
17.
18.
19.
20.

trap	tribe	trick	scrape	sort
trust	trim	sail	gown	post
hundred	press	jail	crowd	brick
brush	check	drill	tower	blind

B. Word Operations Write words from the spelling list to complete the exercises below. If you need help, use the **Spelling Dictionary**.

Operation Past Tense Write the *ed* form of each word.

1. trust   *trusted*

2. blind   ____

3. post   ____

4. tower   ____

5. press   ____

6. check   ____

7. trick   ____

8. crowd   ____

9. drill   ____

10. brush   ____

Operation Plural Write the *s* form of each word.

11. sort   *sorts*

12. hundred   ____

13. trim   ____

14. jail   ____

15. gown   ____

16. scrape   ____

17. brick   ____

18. sail   ____

19. trap   ____

20. tribe   ____

■ bind	★ club	▲ nails	◆ shower	● swim
chase	drag	scrub	slept	sword
climb	highest	share	snap	wait
clown	highway	shell	strike	whip

C. Word Clues Write the spelling word that goes with each clue. The shape after each clue tells you in what column you can find the spelling word. Then write an Other Word Form for each spelling word. If you need help, use the **Spelling Dictionary**.

Word Clues	Spelling Words	Other Word Forms
1. to make a sharp sound ◆	_ _ _ _	___
2. to rub clean ▲	_ _ _ _ _	___
3. to pull along slowly ★	_ _ _ _	___
4. a group of people who meet ★	_ _ _ _	___
5. a hard outer covering ▲	_ _ _ _ _	___
6. to hit ◆	_ _ _ _ _ _	___
7. a strap on a handle ●	_ _ _ _ _	___
8. rested ◆	_ _ _ _ _	___
9. pointed pieces of metal ▲	_ _ _ _ _	___
10. to move in water ●	_ _ _ _	___
11. to tie together ■	_ _ _ _	___
12. to stay in a place ●	_ _ _ _	___
13. a funny circus person ■	_ _ _ _ _	___
14. a bath of spraying water ◆	_ _ _ _ _ _	___
15. to use with others ▲	_ _ _ _ _	___
16. a sharp weapon ●	_ _ _ _ _	___
17. to move upward ■	_ _ _ _ _	___
18. tallest ★	_ _ _ _ _ _ _	___
19. a main road ★	_ _ _ _ _ _ _	___
20. to run after ■	_ _ _ _ _	___

R
E
V
I
E
W

■ bump	★ spend	▲ shout	◆ notebooks	● mostly
o'clock	quite	loud	frame	almost
stocking	fresh	skill	trace	mild
scrap	yellow	again	space	worn

D. Sentences in Paragraphs Write Other Word Forms or the spelling words to complete the sentences. Use the words from the first column to complete the first paragraph, and so on. The shapes will help you match the columns with the paragraphs. Write each word or its Other Word Form only once. If you need help, use the **Spelling Dictionary**.

■ At one **(1.)** __ __ __ __ __ __ in the morning, I crept downstairs in my **(2.)** __ __ __ __ __ __ __ __ feet to the refrigerator. Quietly, I opened the door to see if any **(3.)** __ __ __ __ __ __ of food were there. While reaching for the cheese, I **(4.)** __ __ __ __ __ __ my head and wished I had stayed in bed.

★ In the garden shop, we saw lovely **(5.)** __ __ __ __ __ __ flowers that had been **(6.)** __ __ __ __ __ __ __ **(7.)** cut. They were __ __ __ __ __ beautiful, but we couldn't buy any because we had **(8.)** __ __ __ __ __ all of our money at the movies.

▲ Once **(9.)** __ __ __ __ __ **(10.)** our voices got __ __ __ __ __ __ as we **(11.)** __ __ __ __ __ __ __ and laughed during the math game. Our teacher was pleased to see us using the new **(12.)** __ __ __ __ __ __ we had learned.

◆ I wanted to make a picture **(13.)** __ __ __ __ __ for a drawing I had **(14.)** __ __ __ __ __ __ in my art **(15.)** __ __ __ __ __ __ __ . I had no wood for a real frame. I cut some blue paper and **(16.)** __ __ __ __ __ __ it evenly around my drawing to make a border.

● It is **(17.)** __ __ __ __ __ __ spring, and the **(18.)** __ __ __ __ __ __ weather is coming. I have to **(19.)** __ __ __ __ a coat **(20.)** __ __ __ __ often in the morning when I walk to school.

13

A. Pretest and Proofreading

B. Spelling Words and Phrases

1. bid   will <u>bid</u> at the auction
2. dim   to <u>dim</u> the lights
3. tin   made of <u>tin</u>
4. mix   to <u>mix</u> and pour
5. sixth   <u>sixth</u> time
6. sixteen   <u>sixteen</u> steps to the door
7. mint   flavor of <u>mint</u>
8. mist   hidden in the <u>mist</u>
9. ticket   movie <u>ticket</u>
10. chart   a temperature <u>chart</u>
11. March   a windy <u>March</u>
12. marble   <u>marble</u> floors
13. marker   a red <u>marker</u>
14. farther   <u>farther</u> away
15. reward   collected the <u>reward</u>
16. plane   taking a <u>plane</u>
17. replace   will <u>replace</u> the book
18. skating   <u>skating</u> party

Other Word Forms

bids, bidding, bidder	Mar.
dims, dimmed, dimming, dimmer, dimmest, dimly	marbles, marbled, marbling
tins, tinned	mark, marks, marked, marking
mixes, mixed, mixing, mixer	far, farthest
six, sixths	rewards, rewarded, rewarding
sixteenth	planes
mints, minted, minting	replaces, replaced, replacing
mists, misted, misting, misty	skate, skated, skater
tickets, ticketed, ticketing	
charts, charted, charting	

C. Visual Warm-up

Write the spelling word for each shape.

a.
b.
c.
d.
e.
f.
g.
h.
i.
j.
k.
l.
m.
n.
o.
p.
q.
r.

D. Word Match-ups Find a word in the spelling list that best fits each phrase. Write each word. Check your answers in the **Spelling Dictionary**.

1. a winter sport
2. to stir together
3. flies in the air
4. the third month
5. twelve plus four
6. a crayon
7. light rain
8. a flavorful plant
9. before the seventh

10. not nearer
11. to make an offer
12. a round glass toy
13. to make darker
14. to fill the place of
15. metal for cans
16. a movie pass
17. a prize
18. a map

E. All in a Row Write the eighteen spelling words in alphabetical order. The join the boxed letters and write four hidden words.

1. ☐ _ _
2. _ _ ☐ _ _
3. _ ☐ _
4. _ _ _ ☐ _ _ _
5. Hidden Word =

6. _ _ _ ☐ _ _
7. _ ☐ _ _ _
8. _ _ ☐ _ _ _
9. _ _ ☐ _ _
10. _ _ ☐ _
11. Hidden Word =

12. ☐ _ _
13. _ _ ☐ _ _
14. _ _ _ ☐ _ _ _
15. _ ☐ _ _ _ _
16. Hidden Word =

17. ☐ _ _ _ _ _ _
18. _ _ _ ☐ _
19. _ _ ☐ _ _ _
20. _ ☐ _ _ _
21. _ _ ☐
22. Hidden Word =

Spelling Words

bid	dim	tin	mix	sixth	sixteen
mint	mist	ticket	chart	March	marble
marker	farther	reward	plane	replace	skating

F. Solve the Puzzle Solve the puzzle by using words from the spelling list. Write each word. Check your answers in the **Spelling Dictionary**.

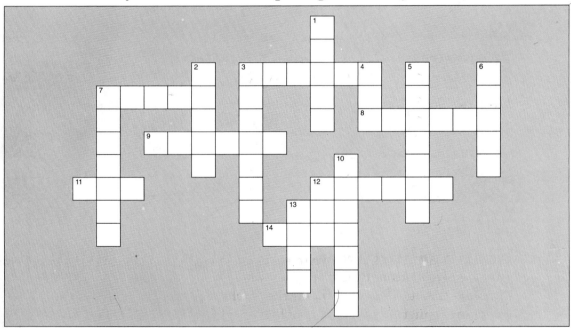

Across

3. money given for information
7. after the fifth
8. something that holds your place
9. a round plaything
11. to offer to pay a certain price
12. a tag or label
13. to stir
14. a plant used for flavoring

Down

1. aircraft
2. a graph or map
3. to take the place of
4. not bright
5. at a greater distance
6. a month
7. gliding on ice
10. eight plus eight
12. a silvery metal
13. a bath of spraying water

G. Using Other Word Forms Write the Other Word Form that completes each sentence.

Base Words: ~~mist(y)~~ mix(ed) bid(ing) ~~dim(er)~~ ~~replace(ing)~~

1. They were _____ the old wallpaper.
2. Because of the light rain, it was a _____ morning.
3. As the sun set, it grew _____ in the woods.
4. The vegetables in the salad were _____ together.
5. They were not _____ at the auction.

H. Challenge Words Write the Challenge Word that completes each phrase.

labels	fifteen	cartons	harness	spacecraft

1. either boxes or _____
2. either an airplane or a _____
3. either fourteen or _____
4. either a leash or a _____
5. either tags or _____

I. Spelling and Writing Write each set of words in a sentence. You may use Other Word Forms. Proofread your work.

1. bid – ticket
2. plane – mist
3. sixth – March
4. marble – reward
5. marker – chart
6. farther – sixteen
7. mix – mint
8. dim – replace
9. tin – skating
10. labels – cartons
11. fifteen – spacecraft
12. harness – replaced

14

A. Pretest and Proofreading

B. Spelling Words and Phrases

1.	oil	motor <u>oil</u>
2.	boil	will <u>boil</u> the water
3.	soil	dark, wet <u>soil</u>
4.	join	if they <u>join</u> us
5.	coin	flipped a <u>coin</u>
6.	noise	a sudden <u>noise</u>
7.	point	<u>point</u> of the story
8.	sliced	<u>sliced</u> tomatoes
9.	sliding	a <u>sliding</u> door
10.	driving	<u>driving</u> carefully
11.	shining	<u>shining</u> the floor
12.	writer	sky <u>writer</u>
13.	river	a winding <u>river</u>
14.	deliver	a load to <u>deliver</u>
15.	silver	<u>silver</u> and gold
16.	women	several <u>women</u>
17.	Wednesday	next <u>Wednesday</u>
18.	September	the first of <u>September</u>

Other Word Forms

oils, oiled, oiling, oily
boils, boiled, boiling,
  boiler
soils, soiled, soiling
joins, joined, joining
coins, coined, coining
noisy, noisier, noisiest,
  noisily
points, pointed, pointing,
  pointer
slice, slices, slicing, slicer
slide, slid, slider

drive, drives, drove
shine, shines, shone,
  shined, shiny
write, writes, wrote,
  writing, written
rivers
delivers, delivered,
  delivering, delivery
silvery
woman, womanly
Wed.
Sept.

C. Visual Warm-up

Write the spelling
word for each shape.

a.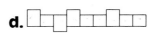

b.

c.

d.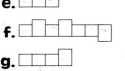

e.

f.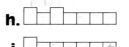

g.

h.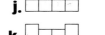

i.

j.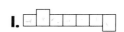

k.

l.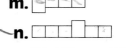

m.

n.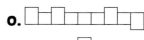

o.

p.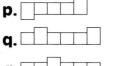

q.

r.

D. Sort Your Words

Write the spelling words under the correct headings. Check your answers in the **Spelling Dictionary**. You will have two words left over.

Words with a Short *i* Sound		Words with a Long *i* Sound		Words with an *oi* Sound	
1. ____	3. ____	5. ____	8. ____	10. ____	14. ____
2. ____	4. ____	6. ____	9. ____	11. ____	15. ____
		7. ____		12. ____	16. ____
				13. ____	

17. Write the two leftover words.

E. Word Operations

As a word doctor, you must change some words before adding a suffix. Make the changes that are needed and write the new words. Some words will not need a change.

	Word	Suffix	New Word
1.	boil	er	____
2.	join	ing	____
3.	write	er	____
4.	deliver	ing	____
5.	slice	ed	____
6.	point	ed	____
7.	drive	ing	____
8.	soil	ed	____
9.	shine	ing	____
10.	oil	ing	____
11.	slide	ing	____
12.	coin	ed	____

Spelling Words

oil	boil	soil	join	coin
noise	point	sliced	sliding	driving
shining	writer	river	deliver	silver
women	Wednesday	September		

F. Word Swap Use the spelling words and Other Word Forms (p. 56) to replace the underlined words or phrases. Write the words.

On the second **(1.)** Tuesday of **(2.)** January, six **(3.)** men stepped into the **(4.)** sparkling bus. The conductor **(5.)** aimed his fingers at a box and asked the people to put their **(6.)** whitish **(7.)** dimes into it. There was so much **(8.)** loud sound that the driver stopped **(9.)** making the bus move. The bus began **(10.)** skidding on a puddle of **(11.)** slime and just missed going into a **(12.)** lake. A **(13.)** person who makes up stories was on his way to **(14.)** bring his story to town. He **(15.)** got together with some people from the bus. One woman showed him the **(16.)** dirt they had landed in. Then she dropped her package of **(17.)** cooked, **(18.)** carved meat. The bus was soon towed.

G. Be a Word Detective The same two vowels are missing from each of the words below. Write the words.

1. s __ __ l

2. b __ __ l

3. p __ __ nt

4. j __ __ n

5. c __ __ n

6. n __ __ se

7. __ __ l

H. Using Other Word Forms
Add an ending to each word to write an Other Word Form.

1. oil + y = ____
2. deliver + y = ____
3. shine + y = ____
4. noise + y = ____
5. slice + ing = ____

I. Challenge Words
Write the Challenge Word that completes each word pair.

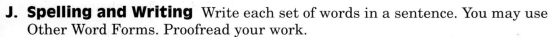

elbow	moist	driver	shivers	wedding

1. knee or ____
2. marriage or ____
3. passenger or ____
4. trembles or ____
5. damp or ____

J. Spelling and Writing
Write each set of words in a sentence. You may use Other Word Forms. Proofread your work.

1. river – noise
2. September – Wednesday
3. sliced – boil
4. oil – soil
5. writer – point
6. shining – coin
7. driving – deliver
8. women – join
9. sliding – silver
10. wedding – driver
11. moist – shivers
12. elbow – slid

A. Pretest and Proofreading

B. Spelling Words and Phrases

1.	dawn	just before dawn
2.	lawn	a lawn mower
3.	laws	passed new laws
4.	draw	had to draw straws
5.	straw	a bale of straw
6.	lean	to lean against
7.	meal	finished the meal
8.	weak	a weak voice
9.	fears	often fears danger
10.	earn	whatever we earn
11.	early	early the next day
12.	earth	the rotation of the earth
13.	heard	heard an echo
14.	heart	a valentine heart
15.	hammer	a hammer and a nail
16.	matter	doesn't matter
17.	madder	madder than ever
18.	ladder	up the ladder

Other Word Forms

dawns, dawned, dawning
lawns
law, lawful, lawyer
draws, drew, drawing,
    drawer
straws
leans, leaned, leaning
meals
weaker, weakest, weakly
fear, feared, fearing, fearful
earns, earned, earning

earlier, earliest
earthy, earthly
hear, hears, hearing
hearts, hearty, heartier,
    heartiest
hammers, hammered,
    hammering
matters
mad, maddest, madly
ladders

C. Visual Warm-up

Write the spelling word for each shape.

a.
b.
c.
d.
e.
f.
g.
h.
i.
j.
k.
l.
m.
n.
o.
p.
q.
r.

D. Missing Vowels Find the missing vowels and write the spelling words.

1. l __ __ n
2. __ __ rl __
3. d __ wn
4. h __ mm __ r
5. l __ dd __ r
6. dr __ w
7. m __ dd __ r
8. m __ tt __ r
9. h __ __ rd

10. l __ wn
11. __ __ rn
12. h __ __ rt
13. str __ w
14. __ __ rth
15. m __ __ l
16. l __ ws
17. w __ __ k
18. f __ __ rs

E. Base Words The spelling list contains fourteen base words and four words that are not base words. Write each spelling word.

Words That Are Not Base Words	Base Words		Words That Are Not Base Words	Base Words
1. earning	_____		10. heartiest	_____
2. earliest	_____		11. straws	_____
3. meals	_____		12. leaning	_____
4. matters	_____		13. drew	_____
5. dawning	_____		14. earthly	_____
6. ladders	_____		15. _____	hear
7. weakly	_____		16. _____	mad
8. hammering	_____		17. _____	fear
9. lawns	_____		18. _____	law

Spelling Words

dawn	*lawn*	*laws*	*draw*	*straw*	*lean*
meal	*weak*	*fears*	*earn*	*early*	*earth*
heard	*heart*	*hammer*	*matter*	*madder*	*ladder*

F. Rearrange and Change How fast can you rearrange the scrambled words to make all of the spelling words? Ask a partner to time you. You must write each word. Ready? Begin! Be sure to time yourself and record your time.

1. wnad	**2.** wadr	**3.** wastr	**4.** rthae	**5.** ealm	**6.** neal
7. redlad	**8.** arne	**9.** yearl	**10.** searf	**11.** keaw	**12.** awls
13. remham	**14.** tremat	**15.** harde	**16.** awnl	**17.** dremad	**18.** thear

G. Using Other Word Forms Write the Other Word Form that fits each series.

Base Words: fear(ing)   hammer(ing)   weak(est)   hearty(est)   draw(ing)

1. draws, drew, _____

2. fears, feared, _____

3. hammers, hammered, _____

4. weak, weaker, _____

5. hearty, heartier, _____

H. Challenge Words Write the Challenge Word that completes each phrase.

earlier	balcony	salad	shawl	seize

1. either a porch or a _____

2. either a scarf or a _____

3. either sooner or _____

4. either vegetables or a _____

5. either grab or _____

I. Spelling and Writing Use each phrase in a sentence. You may want to use the words in a different order or use Other Word Forms. Proofread for spelling using one of the Proofreading Tips.

1. <u>dawn</u> of a new day

2. seeded the <u>lawn</u>

3. <u>laws</u> of nature

4. <u>draw</u> up a will

5. a drinking <u>straw</u>

6. <u>lean</u> meat

7. <u>meal</u> ground from corn

8. a <u>weak</u> battery

9. <u>fears</u> heights

10. <u>earn</u> good grades

11. an <u>early</u> dinner

12. fell to the <u>earth</u>

13. <u>heard</u> the news

14. knows by <u>heart</u>

15. <u>hammer</u> each nail

16. reading <u>matter</u>

17. <u>madder</u> than a wet hen

18. climbing the <u>ladder</u>

16

A. Pretest and Proofreading

B. Spelling Words and Phrases

1.	death	sudden death
2.	breath	out of breath
3.	ahead	far ahead
4.	thread	needle and thread
5.	already	already there
6.	wear	will wear a coat
7.	lightly	stepped lightly
8.	lightning	flash of lightning
9.	broke	broke in two
10.	globe	the spinning globe
11.	froze	froze solid
12.	November	the end of November
13.	score	the winning score
14.	porch	under the porch
15.	Tuesday	Tuesday afternoon
16.	music	distant music
17.	few	a few children
18.	during	during the morning

Other Word Forms

deaths, deathly
breaths, breathed,
  breathing, breathless
threads, threading
wears, wore, worn,
  wearing
light, lights, lit, lighting,
  lighter, lightest
break, breaks, breaking,
  broken

globes, global
freeze, freezes, frozen,
  freezing
Nov.
scores, scoring
porches
Tues.
musical, musically,
  musician
fewer, fewest

C. Visual Warm-up

Write the spelling word for each shape.

a.
b.
c.
d.
e.
f.
g.
h.
i.
j.
k.
l.
m.
n.
o.
p.
q.
r.

D. Word Match-ups Find a word in the spelling list that best fits each word or phrase below. Write the words. Check your answers in the **Spelling Dictionary**.

1. in front
2. the total of points in a game
3. a model of the earth
4. an autumn month
5. thin string
6. to have clothing on
7. screened-in room
8. notes and scales
9. a weekday
10. made cold and solid
11. at some point of time
12. not many
13. goes with thunder
14. air taken into the body
15. came apart
16. softly
17. the end of life
18. by this time

E. Word Clues Be a detective. Study the clues to uncover the words from the spelling list. Write the words.

1. clef, note, staff, conductor, _____
2. dark, stormy, thunder, flash, _____
3. Thanksgiving, cold, football, month, _____
4. weekday, school, work, study, _____
5. chairs, front, house, outside, _____
6. team, goal, points, touchdown, _____
7. earth, round, equator, axis, _____
8. tailor, sew, needle, stitch, _____
9. gasp, inhale, air, oxygen, _____

Spelling Words

death	breath	ahead	thread	already
wear	tightly	lightning	broke	globe
froze	November	score	porch	Tuesday
music	few	during		

F. Guide Words These word pairs are guide words that might appear in a dictionary. Write the words from the spelling list that would appear on the same page as each pair of guide words.

Example:

huge – kept

hunter

iron

above – ax

1. _____ 2. _____

blame – bucket

3. _____ 4. _____

correct – dirt

5. _____

dirty – evening

6. _____

event – flock

7. _____

floor – gang

8. _____

get – hate

9. _____

leaf – lucky

10. _____ 11. _____

mean – nineteen

12. _____

nobody – outfit

13. _____

pocket – purse

14. _____

scale – sheet

15. _____

stream – thread

16. _____

throw – unlock

17. _____

until – worry

18. _____

G. Using Other Word Forms Write the Other Word Form that fits each clue.

Base Words: break(ing) breath(less) score(ing) light(ing) globe(al)

1. short of breath
2. making points in a game
3. all over the world
4. destroying
5. adding light to an area

H. Challenge Words Write the Challenge Word that completes each question.

beauty	duty	fuel	insure	stored

1. What type of _____ is used to heat the house?
2. Where is the furniture _____ ?
3. Is there _____ in a sunset?
4. Should ___ my car against collision damage?
5. Who has a _____ to perform?

I. Spelling and Writing Write each set of words in a sentence. You may use Other Word Forms. Proofread your work.

1. lightly – music
2. few – breath
3. wear – froze
4. lightning – ahead
5. score – during
6. Tuesday – November
7. broke – globe
8. porch – thread
9. already – death
10. duty – insure
11. fuel – stored
12. beauty – breathless

17

A. Pretest and Proofreading

B. Spelling Words and Phrases

1.	until	until you come
2.	study	tried to study
3.	lucky	your lucky charm
4.	bucket	the bucket of cement
5.	number	remembered their number
6.	Sunday	Sunday gathering
7.	sir	sir or madam
8.	shirt	checkered shirt
9.	dirty	dirty clothes
10.	birthday	my next birthday
11.	leaf	a yellow leaf
12.	leak	a leak in the hose
13.	leading	leading the race
14.	heating	heating the water
15.	scold	to scold for nothing
16.	oldest	oldest in the family
17.	holding	holding tighter
18.	poster	baseball poster

Other Word Forms

studies, studied, studying, student, studious
luckier, luckiest, luckily
buckets
numbers, numbered, numbering
Sun.
sirs
shirts
dirtier, dirtiest
birthdays

leaves, leafy
leaks, leaked, leaking, leaky
lead, leads, led
heat, heats, heated, heater
scolds, scolded, scolding
old, older
hold, holds, held
posters

C. Visual Warm-up

Write the spelling word for each shape.

a.
b.
c.
d.
e.
f.
g.
h.
i.
j.
k.
l.
m.
n.
o.
p.
q.
r.

D. Sort Your Words Write each of the spelling words where it belongs.

One-syllable Words	Two-syllable Words		
1. ___	6. ___	11. ___	16. ___
2. ___	7. ___	12. ___	17. ___
3. ___	8. ___	13. ___	18. ___
4. ___	9. ___	14. ___	
5. ___	10. ___	15. ___	

19. By adding endings to the spelling words, make four three-syllable Other Word Forms (p. 68). Write them.

E. Break the Code Use the code to write the spelling words.

1	2	3	4	5	6	7	8	9	10	11	12	13	14	15	16	17	18	19	20
↓	↓	↓	↓	↓	↓	↓	↓	↓	↓	↓	↓	↓	↓	↓	↓	↓	↓	↓	↓
a	b	c	d	e	f	g	h	i	k	l	m	n	o	p	r	s	t	u	y

1. 11, 5, 1, 6

2. 17, 8, 9, 16, 18

3. 4, 9, 16, 18, 20

4. 17, 18, 19, 4, 20

5. 19, 13, 18, 9, 11

6. 17, 3, 14, 11, 4

7. 11, 5, 1, 10

8. 14, 11, 4, 5, 17, 18

9. 17, 9, 16

10. 8, 14, 11, 4, 9, 13, 7

11. 17, 19, 13, 4, 1, 20

12. 15, 14, 17, 18, 5, 16

13. 2, 19, 3, 10, 5, 18

14. 13, 19, 12, 2, 5, 16

15. 11, 19, 3, 10, 20

16. 8, 5, 1, 18, 9, 13, 7

17. 11, 5, 1, 4, 9, 13, 7

18. 2, 9, 16, 18, 8, 4, 1, 20

Spelling Words

until	study	lucky	bucket	number
Sunday	sir	shirt	dirty	birthday
leaf	leak	leading	heating	scold
oldest	holding	poster		

F. Words and Meanings Write a spelling word for each meaning. Check your answers in the **Spelling Dictionary**.

1. a day of the week
2. a thin, flat part of a plant
3. up to the time of
4. a round container for carrying things
5. to try to learn
6. a hole that lets something in or out by accident
7. making warm
8. having lived for the longest time
9. being ahead of
10. a piece of clothing for the upper body
11. the day on which someone is born
12. a large printed notice
13. a numeral connected with a person or thing
14. taking and keeping in one's hands
15. to blame angrily
16. having good fortune
17. unclean
18. a title used instead of a man's name

G. Using Other Word Forms Write the Other Word Form that fits each group of words.

Base Words: leak(y) study(ed) number(ed) lucky(est) leaf(es)

1. bark, trunk, roots, _____
2. faucet, old hose, tire losing air, _____
3. most fortunate, winner, _____
4. examined, books, test, _____
5. put in order, given a place, _____

H. Challenge Words Write the Challenge Word that completes each word pair.

ease	folks	furnish	lumber	alert

1. wide-awake and _____
2. wood and _____
3. people and _____
4. comfort and _____
5. provide and _____

I. Spelling and Writing Write two or more answers to each question. Use as many Spelling Words, Other Word Forms, and Challenge Words as you can. A few words are suggested. Proofread for spelling using one of the Proofreading Tips from the Yellow Pages.

1. How would you plan for a special party?
   lucky   until   birthday   leading   numbered   folks

2. Why does Alan have to change his clothes?
   Sunday   dirtiest   oldest   shirt   heating   alert

3. Why did father laugh when he saw his son?
   holding   bucket   leaking   scolding   study   ease

■ mist	★ early	▲ lightning	◆ September	● wear
mix	heard	Tuesday	Sunday	November
March	lightly	ahead	until	weak
Wednesday	during	already	holding	farther

A. Weather Watch Write Other Word Forms or the spelling words to complete these sentences about weather. The shapes tell you in what column you can find the spelling word. Write each word or its Other Word Form only once. If you need help, use the **Spelling Dictionary**.

1. The snowstorm came ★ _ _ _ _ _ _ _ than we expected.

2. Thunder and ▲ _ _ _ _ _ _ _ _ _ are coming our way.

3. A ■ _ _ _ _ _ fog rolled off the ocean.

4. There were a few sunny days in the month of ◆ _ _ _ _ _ _ _ _ _.

5. You will be ● _ _ _ _ _ _ _ coats tomorrow if it gets colder.

6. For the holiday on ◆ _ _ _ _ _ _ , there will be clear skies.

7. We will be ★ _ _ _ _ _ _ _ thunder later on today.

8. The month of ● _ _ _ _ _ _ _ _ _ was filled with sunny days.

9. Rain ■ _ _ _ _ _ with snow is forecasted.

10. On ▲ _ _ _ _ _ _ _ there is a chance of freezing rain.

11. There will be a ★ _ _ _ _ _ snowfall tonight.

12. As the storm got closer, it got ● _ _ _ _ _ _ in strength.

13. A strong ■ _ _ _ _ _ wind will bend the trees.

14. It will be 24 hours ◆ _ _ _ _ _ the rain stops.

15. The clouds up ▲ _ _ _ _ _ look very dark.

16. The latest map shows the storm moving ● _ _ _ _ _ _ _ _ out to sea.

17. The storm will likely ◆ _ _ _ _ _ off until early evening.

18. By noon today, there ▲ _ _ _ _ _ _ _ _ was flooding in the streets.

19. Children missed school on ■ _ _ _ _ _ _ _ _ _ due to the hurricane.

20. Two feet of snow fell ★ _ _ _ _ _ _ the night.

oil	dawn	lawn	leak	draw
earn	hammer	heart	tin	few
point	join	thread	leaf	breath
deliver	lean	meal	silver	broke

B. Squaring Off Add endings to the spelling words. Write the new words. For some words you need to add or subtract a letter before adding the ending. If you need help, use the **Spelling Dictionary**.

a. Add *ing*

oil

earn

point

deliver

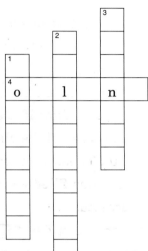

b. Add *s*

lawn

heart

thread

meal

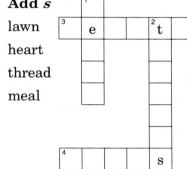

c. Add *ed*

dawn

hammer

join

lean

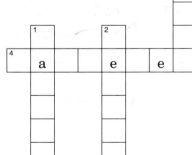

d. Add *y*

leak

tin

leaf

silver

e. Add *er*

draw

few

breath

broke

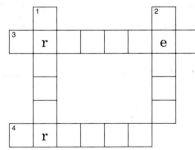

boil	ladder	marker	score	skating
bucket	laws	mint	shirt	sliding
earth	lucky	music	sir	straw
fears	madder	noise	sixteen	women
froze	marble	river	sixth	writer

C. Hidden Words
Use the clues to find Other Word Forms or the spelling words in the puzzle. Write each word.

```
b o i l i n g c m a r b l e s
u p l a d d e r s s i w r m h
c e o w s k a t e d v z d o i
k m n a r j i m t v e b n s r
e a r t h d b i u w r q p e t
t o f e a r x n o r s i x c s
s i x t e e n t h m a d n a m
f r e e z e o m u s i c i a n
b z y q u t i n o s l i d e s
l u c k i e s t r a w y z w i
s c o r e d e m a r k s t b r
w r i t e x s w o m a n c t u
```

11. moved on ice

__ __ __ __ __ __

12. our planet __ __ __ __ __

13. to feel afraid __ __ __ __

14. after five __ __ __

15. after the fifteenth

__ __ __ __ __ __ __ __

16. angry __ __ __

17. to make water into ice

__ __ __ __ __

18. violinist

__ __ __ __ __ __ __

19. moves on a smooth surface

__ __ __ __ __ __ __

20. having the best luck

__ __ __ __ __ __ __

21. stalks of grain __ __ __ __ __

22. made points in a game

__ __ __ __ __ __

23. spots on a paper

__ __ __ __

24. to make words with a pen

__ __ __ __ __

25. an adult female

__ __ __ __ __

Down

1. used to carry sand __ __ __ __ __ __

2. a rule __ __ __

3. unpleasant sounds __ __ __ __ __

4. a plant used for flavoring __ __ __ __

5. streams of water __ __ __ __ __

6. clothing that has sleeves

__ __ __ __ __

7. a title for a man __ __ __

Across

8. bubbling hot __ __ __ __ __ __ __

9. polished round stones

__ __ __ __ __ __ __

10. used for climbing __ __ __ __ __ __

bid	dim	leading	porch	shining
birthday	dirty	matter	poster	sliced
chart	driving	number	replace	soil
coin	globe	oldest	reward	study
death	heating	plane	scold	ticket

D. Word Arithmetic Make one or two changes on each spelling word to write an Other Word Form.

1. replace − e + ing =

2. plane + s =

3. shining − ing + es =

4. number + ed =

5. oldest − est + er =

6. bid + d + er =

7. sliced − ed + ing =

8. death + ly =

9. study − y + ies =

10. poster + s =

11. reward + ed =

12. soil + s =

13. matter + ed =

14. porch + es =

15. heating − ing + ed =

16. dim + ly =

17. coin + ed =

18. globe − e + al =

19. scold + s =

20. birthday + s =

21. chart + ed =

22. ticket + ing =

23. driving − ing + es =

24. leading − ing + s =

25. dirty − y + ier =

WANTED
The Tin Can Caper
Billy Goat
$1 Reward

WANTED
for The Honey Heist
"Grizzly" Bear
$5000 Reward

WANTED
The Great Peanut Robbery
"Dumbo" Elephant
$1,000,001 Reward

19

A. Pretest and Proofreading

B. Spelling Words and Phrases

1. iron ✓ — to iron the clothes
2. island ✓ — small island
3. tiny ✓ — tiny gerbil
4. quiet ✓ — quiet evening
5. Friday ✓ — Friday night
6. provide ✓ — will provide the meal
7. lamb — heard the lamb
8. wrap ✓ — to wrap the package
9. crack ✓ — through the crack
10. crash ✓ — will crash to the floor
11. flash ✓ — done in a flash
12. drank ✓ — drank too fast
13. blanket ✓ — favorite blanket
14. glasses ✓ — wears glasses
15. led ✗ — led them away
16. fled ✗ — fled from the room
17. shed ✓ — hidden in the shed
18. monster ✓ — my pet monster

Other Word Forms

irons, ironed, ironing	flashes, flashed, flashing
islands	drink, drinks, drinking,
tinier, tiniest	drunk
quietly, quieter, quietest	blankets, blanketed,
Fri.	blanketing
provides, provided,	glass, glassy
providing, provider	lead, leads, leading
lambs	flee, flees, fleeing
wraps, wrapped, wrapping	sheds, shedding
cracks, cracked, cracking	monsters, monstrous
crashes, crashed, crashing	

C. Visual Warm-up

Write the spelling word for each shape.

a.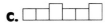

b.

c.

d.

e.

f.

g.

h.

i.

j.

k.

l.

m.

n.

o.

p.

q.

r.

D. Word Match-ups Find a word in the spelling list that best fits each phrase. Write each word. Check your answers in the **Spelling Dictionary**.

1. used to see better
2. ran away
3. land with water all around
4. used on a bed to keep warm
5. an ugly movie character
6. unlucky day when it's 13
7. very small
8. to cover with paper and tie up
9. a little storage building
10. opposite of *followed*
11. a noisy fall
12. without noise
13. swallowed milk
14. a long narrow opening
15. a baby sheep
16. a quick, bright light
17. used to press clothes
18. to give what is needed

Spelling Words

iron	island	tiny	quiet	Friday	provide
lamb	wrap	crack	crash	flash	drank
blanket	glasses	led	fled	shed	monster

E. Base Words The spelling list contains fourteen base words and four words that are not base words. Write each spelling word.

Words That Are Not Base Words	Base Words		Words That Are Not Base Words	Base Words
1. cracking	_____		**10.** quietly	_____
2. Fri.	_____		**11.** flashing	_____
3. blankets	_____		**12.** monsters	_____
4. tinier	_____		**13.** sheds	_____
5. providing	_____		**14.** lambs	_____
6. ironing	_____		**15.** _____	lead
7. wrapped	_____		**16.** _____	drink
8. crashing	_____		**17.** _____	flee
9. islands	_____		**18.** _____	glass

F. Word Hunt The spelling words can be found in the word puzzle. The words appear across and down. Write the words.

```
i r o n l a m b f f
s h e d c s t g l r
l e d w r a p l a i
a b d o a l m a s d
n o e t c r a s h a
d r a n k e r s t y
b l a n k e t e i f
p r o v i d e s n l
p m o n s t e r y e
o s n t q u i e t d
```

Across

1. ⬜⬜⬜⬜
2. ⬜⬜⬜
3. ⬜⬜⬜
4. ⬜⬜
5. ⬜⬜⬜⬜
6. ⬜⬜⬜⬜
7. ⬜⬜⬜⬜
8. ⬜⬜⬜⬜⬜
9. ⬜⬜⬜⬜⬜

10. ⬜⬜⬜⬜⬜⬜
11. ⬜⬜⬜⬜

Down

12. ⬜⬜⬜⬜⬜⬜
13. ⬜⬜⬜⬜⬜
14. ⬜⬜⬜⬜⬜⬜
15. ⬜⬜⬜⬜
16. ⬜⬜⬜⬜
17. ⬜⬜⬜⬜⬜
18. ⬜⬜⬜

G. Using Other Word Forms Write the Other Word Form that completes each sentence.

Base Words: monster(ous) shed(ing) flee(ing) wrap(ed) tiny(est)

1. He was running away. He was ——— .

2. The snake was losing its skin. It was ——— .

3. The gift was covered with paper and a bow. It was ——— .

4. It was the smallest. It was the ——— .

5. The plant was huge. It was ——— .

H. Challenge Words Write the Challenge Word that replaces each underlined word or phrase.

magnet	canned	striking	oddly	dwellings

1. Their <u>homes</u> are made of logs.

2. The animals behaved <u>strangely</u>.

3. The vegetables are <u>in metal containers</u>.

4. It's a <u>thing that attracts iron</u>.

5. What were you <u>hitting</u>?

I. Spelling and Writing Write each set of words in a sentence. You may use Other Word Forms. Proofread your work.

1. led – monster

2. wrap – shed

3. provide – lamb

4. flash – island

5. fled – crash

6. quiet – drank

7. blanket – tiny

8. crack – glasses

9. Friday – iron

10. magnet – striking

11. dwellings – canned

12. oddly – monsters

20

A. Pretest and Proofreading

B. Spelling Words and Phrases

1. beef — all beef frankfurt
2. heel — heel of my boot
3. sheep — frolicking sheep
4. steep — down the steep path
5. agree — if you agree
6. cheer — stood up to cheer
7. jar — jar of cream
8. yard — in the front yard
9. harm — no harm done
10. party — invited to the party
11. partly — partly completed
12. candle — lighted candle
13. handle — broom handle
14. paddle — will paddle up the stream
15. saddle — an old western saddle
16. banner — the school banner
17. battle — a battle for first place
18. cattle — cattle on the range

Other Word Forms

beefy	part, parts, parted, parting
heels, heeled	
sheepish	candles
steeper, steepest	handles, handled, handling
agrees, agreed, agreeing, agreeable	paddles, paddled, paddling
cheers, cheered, cheering, cheery, cheerful	saddles, saddled, saddling
jars, jarred, jarring	banners
yards	battles, battled, battling
harms, harmed, harming, harmful	
parties, partying	

C. Visual Warm-up

Write the spelling word for each shape.

a. ☐☐☐☐
b. ☐☐☐
c. ☐☐☐☐☐
d. ☐☐☐☐☐
e. ☐☐☐☐☐☐
f. ☐☐☐☐☐☐
g. ☐☐☐☐☐☐☐
h. ☐☐☐☐
i. ☐☐☐☐
j. ☐☐☐☐☐☐
k. ☐☐☐☐☐☐
l. ☐☐☐☐☐
m. ☐☐☐☐☐
n. ☐☐☐☐☐
o. ☐☐☐☐☐
p. ☐☐☐☐☐☐
q. ☐☐☐☐☐☐
r. ☐☐☐☐☐

D. Words and Meanings Write a spelling word for each meaning. Check your answers in the **Spelling Dictionary**.

1. an animal with thick wool and hooves
2. an area of ground around a house
3. meat from cattle
4. a fight
5. to give a happy shout
6. having an almost straight up-and-down slope
7. the part of an object held by the hand
8. to think the same as another
9. a seat for riding on a horse
10. part of a shoe
11. a flag
12. to move a canoe with an oar
13. cows and bulls
14. a glass or clay container
15. in part
16. a stick of wax with a wick
17. people gathered to have fun
18. damage or injury

E. Hinky Pinky The solution to each Hinky Pinky is two rhyming words, each with two syllables. Solve each Hinky Pinky. At least one word of each Hinky Pinky will be a spelling word. Write your answers.

Example: This is very strong tall building. _____*power tower*_____

1. This holds something that gives light in darkness.
2. Two cows' fighting is called this.
3. This is an event for bright people.
4. A riding cowboy uses this to budge his horse.
5. This is a person who plans a pattern for a flag.

Spelling Words

beef	*heel*	*sheep*	*steep*	*agree*	*cheer*
jar	*yard*	*harm*	*party*	*partly*	*candle*
handle	*paddle*	*saddle*	*banner*	*battle*	*cattle*

F. Sort Your Words In alphabetical order, write the spelling words where they belong.

Words with an *ar*		Words with Two *e*'s		Words with an *le* Ending	
1. _____	4. _____	6. _____	9. _____	12. _____	15. _____
2. _____	5. _____	7. _____	10. _____	13. _____	16. _____
3. _____		8. _____	11. _____	14. _____	17. _____

18. Write the one word not used above.

G. Break the Code Use the code to write the spelling words.

a	b	c	d	e	f	g	h	i	j	k	l	m
↕	↕	↕	↕	↕	↕	↕	↕	↕	↕	↕	↕	↕
z	y	x	w	v	u	t	s	r	q	p	o	n

1. xzmwov

2. kzwwov

3. qzi

4. xzggov

5. szin

6. ztivv

7. svvo

8. yzmmvi

9. kzigb

10. xsvvi

11. hzwwov

12. kzigob

13. yzggov

14. hsvvk

15. hgvvk

16. szmwov

17. bziw

18. yvvu

H. Using Other Word Forms Write the Other Word Form that fits each series.

Base Words: handle(ing) saddle(ing) battle(ing) jar(ed) paddle(ing)

1. jars, _____ , jarring
2. paddles, paddled, _____
3. saddles, saddled, _____
4. battles, battled, _____
5. handles, handled, _____

I. Challenge Words Write the Challenge Word that completes each phrase.

nearly	rattlesnake	scarlet	harmless	zebra

1. either red or _____
2. either almost or _____
3. either a cobra or a _____
4. either a horse or a _____
5. either safe or _____

J. Spelling and Writing Write two or more questions about each statement. Use as many Spelling Words, Other Word Forms, and Challenge Words as you can. A few words are suggested. Proofread for spelling using one of the Proofreading Tips from the Yellow Pages.

1. Parties can be fun.
party banner candle cheering yard partly
Example: Did they string a <u>party</u> <u>banner</u> across the front <u>yard</u>?

2. Movies about the Old West can be exciting.
sheep cattle beef steep paddle saddle jarring rattlesnake

3. The large dog was quite friendly.
agree heel harmless handle battle nearly

21

A. Pretest and Proofreading

B. Spelling Words and Phrases

1.	ton	a ton of coal
2.	job	another job
3.	sob	a frightened sob
4.	fond	fond of swimming
5.	chop	a thick lamb chop
6.	copy	will copy over again
7.	bother	doesn't bother me
8.	wrong	wrong time
9.	strong	strong harness
10.	belonged	belonged together
11.	burn	if it will burn
12.	nurse	the night nurse
13.	purse	found my purse
14.	turtle	the sunning turtle
15.	returning	returning the books
16.	sure	is sure of the answer
17.	grind	to grind the grain
18.	remind	if you remind me

Other Word Forms

tons	burns, burned, burning,
jobs	burner
sobs, sobbed, sobbing	nurses, nursed, nursing
fonder, fondest, fondly	purses
chops, chopped,	turtles
chopping	return, returns, returned
copies, copied, copying	surest, surely
bothers, bothered, bothering	grinds, ground, grinding,
wronged, wrongly	grinder
strongly, stronger, strongest	reminds, reminded,
belong, belongs, belonging,	reminding
belongings	

C. Visual Warm-up

Write the spelling word for each shape.

a.

b.

c.

d.

e.

f.

g.

h.

i.

j.

k.

l.

m.

n.

o.

p.

q.

r.

D. Bases and Suffixes The spelling list contains sixteen base words and two words with suffixes. Write each spelling word.

Words with Suffixes	Base Words		Words with Suffixes	Base Words
1. tons	___	**10.** sobbing	___
2. nursing	___	**11.** bothering	___
3. jobs	___	**12.** reminding	___
4. chopping	___	**13.** fondest	___
5. copies	___	**14.** grinding	___
6. surest	___	**15.** burner	___
7. purses	___	**16.** wrongly	___
8. turtles	___	**17.** ___	belong
9. strongest	___	**18.** ___	return

E. Guide Words These word pairs are guide words that might appear in a dictionary. Write the words from the spelling list that would appear on the same page as each pair of guide words.

backward – bucket
1. ___   **2.** ___

build – change
3. ___

chart – corner
4. ___   **5.** ___

floor – gang
6. ___

get – kept
7. ___   **8.** ___

nobody – outfit
9. ___

pocket – purse
10. ___

queen – return
11. ___

returning – saves
12. ___

sob – thread
13. ___   **15.** ___
14. ___

throw – unlock
16. ___   **17.** ___

worth – yellow
18. ___

Spelling Words

ton	job	sob	fond	chop
copy	bother	wrong	strong	belonged
burn	nurse	purse	turtle	returning
sure	grind	remind		

F. Crossword Puzzle Solve the puzzle by using words from the spelling list. Write the words. Check your answers in the **Spelling Dictionary**.

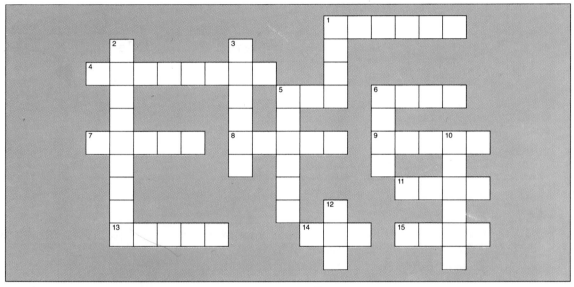

Across

1. to trouble or pester
4. was a member of
5. 2,000 pounds
6. to cut with a sharp tool
7. the opposite of *right*
8. a hospital worker
9. a container for money
11. certain
13. to make into powder
14. work that has to be done
15. loving or liking

Down

1. pain from a fire
2. coming back
3. to make someone remember
5. a slow animal
6. one of many of the same
10. not weak
12. to cry

G. Using Other Word Forms Write the Other Word Form that completes each sentence.

Base Words: fond(ly)   copy(ed)   remind(ing)   chop(ing)   sob(ing)

1. The child was _____ after the fall.

2. I am always _____ myself to do things.

3. The cook was _____ the vegetables.

4. The student _____ the word incorrectly.

5. The doe looked _____ at her fawn.

H. Challenge Words Write the Challenge Word that fits each clue.

coffee	turf	bothered	title	turkey

1. the name of a book

2. a Thanksgiving treat

3. a flavor of ice cream

4. the surface layer of grass

5. annoyed or irritated

I. Spelling and Writing Write each set of words in a sentence. You may use Other Word Forms. Proofread your work.

1. nurse – burn

2. sob – purse

3. strong – ton

4. fond – belonged

5. copy – bother

6. sure – remind

7. turtle – returning

8. grind – chop

9. wrong – job

10. coffee – bothered

11. turkey – turf

12. title – copied

22

A. Pretest and Proofreading

B. Spelling Words and Phrases

1. real — the <u>real</u> thing
2. seat — on the back <u>seat</u>
3. team — the winning <u>team</u>
4. tear — <u>tear</u> in my eye
5. feeling — <u>feeling</u> better
6. meeting — attended the <u>meeting</u>
7. weekend — next <u>weekend</u>
8. between — <u>between</u> two slices of bread
9. coal — lump of hard <u>coal</u>
10. coach — the football <u>coach</u>
11. chose — <u>chose</u> a partner
12. phone — answered the <u>phone</u>
13. stole — if they <u>stole</u> it
14. smoke — smell of <u>smoke</u>
15. spoke — <u>spoke</u> harshly
16. sport — my favorite <u>sport</u>
17. shore — drifted into <u>shore</u>
18. stories — has read more <u>stories</u>

Other Word Forms

really	phones, phoned, phoning
seats, seated, seating	steal, steals, stealing,
teams	stolen
tears, teared, tearing,	smokes, smoked,
tearful	smoking, smoky
feel, feels, felt	speak, speaks, spoken,
meet, meets, met	speaking, speaker
weekends	sports
coals	shores
coaches, coached, coaching	story
choose, chooses, chosen,	
choosing	

C. Visual Warm-up

Write the spelling word for each shape.

a.
b.
c.
d.
e.
f.
g.
h.
i.
j.
k.
l.
m.
n.
o.
p.
q.
r.

D. All in a Row Write the eighteen spelling words in alphabetical order. Then join the boxed letters and write four hidden words.

1. _ _ _ ☐ _ _ _
2. _ ☐ _ _ _ _
3. _ _ ☐ _ _
4. _ _ _ ☐
5. _ _ ☐ _ _ _
6. Hidden Word =

7. ☐ _ _ _ _ _ _
8. _ _ _ _ ☐
9. _ _ ☐ _
10. _ _ _ ☐
11. Hidden Word =

12. _ ☐ _ _ _
13. _ _ ☐ _ _
14. _ _ ☐ _ _
15. _ ☐ _ _ _
16. ☐ _ _ _ _ _
17. Hidden Word =

18. ☐ _ _ _ _ _ _
19. _ ☐ _ _
20. _ ☐ _ _
21. _ _ _ _ _ _ ☐
22. Hidden Word =

E. Base Words The spelling list contains twelve base words and six words that are not base words. Write each spelling word.

Words That Are Not Base Words	Base Words		Words That Are Not Base Words	Base Words
1. teams	_____		10. coaches	_____
2. sports	_____		11. tearing	_____
3. seating	_____		12. _____	feel
4. shores	_____		13. _____	meet
5. really	_____		14. _____	story
6. smoking	_____		15. _____	steal
7. coals	_____		16. _____	choose
8. phoned	_____		17. _____	speak
9. weekends	_____			

18. Write the one base word not used above.

Spelling Words

real	seat	team	tear	feeling	meeting
weekend	between	coal	coach	chose	phone
stole	smoke	spoke	sport	shore	stories

F. Out of Order The underlined word in each sentence does not make sense because the letters in it are out of order. Rearrange the letters so the sentence makes sense. Write the word change.

1. The <u>stea</u> must be painted again.
2. Children enjoy <u>rosties</u> and fairy tales.
3. Baseball is a popular <u>rtosp</u>.
4. The <u>eamt</u> had a winning season.
5. A <u>eart</u> ran down my face.
6. Is that jewel fake or <u>aler</u>?
7. Clams are found near the <u>reosh</u>.
8. He <u>keosp</u> about your problem.
9. Who <u>secho</u> the winner?
10. I will rake the leaves this <u>ndekewe</u>.
11. Who is the team's <u>choac</u>?
12. Why are you <u>englife</u> sad?
13. The thief <u>lesto</u> my car.
14. The <u>nepho</u> did not ring.
15. She wrote <u>tweeben</u> the lines.
16. The <u>engtime</u> will come to order.
17. Thick <u>kesmo</u> rose from the chimney.
18. You can burn <u>laco</u> in this stove.

G. Using Other Word Forms Write the Other Word Form that is the opposite of each word.

Base Words: tear(ful) real(ly) choose(ing) speak(er) coach(es)

1. players

2. assigning

3. joyful

4. listener

5. not actually

H. Challenge Words Write the Challenge Word that completes each group of words.

roasting	codes	hoarse	fleeing	series

1. signals, dots and dashes, secret, _____

2. husky voice, sore throat, _____

3. cooking, baking, oven, _____

4. escaping, running away, _____

5. set, group of stories, television, _____

I. Spelling and Writing Write *two* or more answers to each question. Use as many Spelling Words, Other Word Forms, and Challenge Words as you can. A few words are suggested. Proofread your work.

1. What might happen if you were cooking a meal on the grill and you burned everything?

feeling – hoarse – smoke – coal – roasting

2. What would you do if you were leading in a big race and someone passed you just before you crossed the finish line?

meeting – weekend – team – sport – coach

3. What would you say to the principal if you couldn't find your bicycle in the schoolyard?

stole – phone – codes – spoke – fleeing

23

A. Pretest and Proofreading

B. Spelling Words and Phrases

1.	alone	was never <u>alone</u>
2.	awoke	<u>awoke</u> early
3.	glow	the <u>glow</u> of the fire
4.	golden	<u>golden</u> sunset
5.	rolled	<u>rolled</u> across the floor
6.	hoping	<u>hoping</u> to go
7.	nobody	but <u>nobody</u> called
8.	greet	will <u>greet</u> them at the door
9.	teeth	brushed my <u>teeth</u>
10.	indeed	was <u>indeed</u> welcome
11.	event	next <u>event</u>
12.	level	made it <u>level</u>
13.	clever	<u>clever</u> stunt
14.	eleven	<u>eleven</u> and one
15.	seventh	the <u>seventh</u> child
16.	laugh	had to <u>laugh</u>
17.	January	a <u>January</u> storm
18.	Saturday	going away <u>Saturday</u>

Other Word Forms

awake, awakes, awaking, awoken	events, eventful
glows, glowed, glowing	levels, leveled, leveling
gold	cleverer, cleverest
roll, rolls, rolling, roller	eleventh
hope, hopes, hoped, hopeful, hopefully	seven
greets, greeted, greeting	laughs, laughed, laughing, laughable
tooth, toothy	Jan.
	Sat.

C. Visual Warm-up

Write the spelling word for each shape.

a.
b.
c.
d.
e.
f.
g.
h.
i.
j.
k.
l.
m.
n.
o.
p.
q.
r.

D. Find the Missing Treasure Unscramble the letters in the footprints and discover all the spelling words. Write the words.

1. vercle
2. pihong
3. theet
4. aaurnyJ
5. ghaul
6. vente
7. yoodnb
8. veeenl
9. wogl
10. doller
11. veell
12. nthseev
13. egret
14. naloe
15. koaew
16. durtaayS
17. deined
18. neldog

E. Word Search The spelling words can be found in the puzzle. The words appear across and down. Write the words.

Across

1.
2.
3.
4.
5.
6.
7.
8.
9.
10.

Down

11.
12.
13.
14.
15.
16.
17.
18.

```
a s a t u r d a y t t i
w g l o w o g r e e t n
o n w v o l a u g h l d
k c l e v e r t o o b e
e l e v e n x n l p n e
a s v e e c d o d i o d
l i e n z y c d e n b o
o l l t e e t h n g o f
n r o l l e d f x u d n
e o p r j a n u a r y s
t o s e v e n t h o p o
```

Spelling Words

alone	awoke	glow	golden	rolled
hoping	nobody	greet	teeth	indeed
event	level	clever	eleven	seventh
laugh	January	Saturday		

F. Words and Meanings Write a spelling word for each meaning. Check your answers in the **Spelling Dictionary**.

1. bright-yellow
2. turned over and over
3. by oneself
4. no person
5. to welcome in a friendly way
6. light made by a fire
7. to make sounds that show happiness
8. woke up
9. really
10. a day of the week
11. skillful
12. the first month in the year
13. wishing
14. after the sixth
15. one more than ten
16. more than one tooth
17. at an equal height
18. a contest in a sports program

G. Using Other Word Forms Write the Other Word Form that completes each phrase.

Base Words: hope(ful) level(ing) awake(ing) event(ful) laugh(ing)

1. not boring, but _____

2. not hopeless, but _____

3. not making uneven, but _____

4. not crying, but _____

5. not falling asleep, but _____

H. Challenge Words Write the Challenge Word that fits each question.

crackers	theme	greeting	eleventh	spoken

1. Are oral stories always _____?

2. Who's the _____ member of the football team?

3. Who is _____ the guests?

4. What is the _____ of your story?

5. Do you like _____ with peanut butter?

I. Spelling and Writing Write each set of words in a sentence. You may use Other Word Forms. Proofread your work.

1. laugh – rolled

2. glow – golden

3. nobody – clever

4. indeed – alone

5. event – level

6. hoping – seventh

7. greet – eleven

8. January – awoke

9. teeth – Saturday

10. spoken – greeting

11. eleventh – crackers

12. theme – laughed

24

■ iron	★ January	▲ island	◆ blanket	● sheep
nurse	banner	party	candle	weekend
team	coach	event	flash	stories
phone	shed	Friday	purse	teeth

A. What's the Name Write Other Word Forms or the spelling words to name the items below. The shapes tell you in what column you can find the spelling word. Write each word or its Other Word Form only once. If you need help, use the **Spelling Dictionary**.

1. You use these to keep warm on cold nights. ◆ _ _ _ _ _ _ _ _

2. This month begins a new year. ★ _ _ _ _ _ _ _

3. These animals grow thick wool. ● _ _ _ _ _

4. These are heated and used to press clothing. ■ _ _ _ _ _

5. These lands are surrounded by water. ▲ _ _ _ _ _ _

6. They light up a birthday cake. ◆ _ _ _ _ _ _

7. You buy these flags at baseball games. ★ _ _ _ _ _ _ _

8. They care for sick people. ■ _ _ _ _ _ _

9. This is the end of every week. ● _ _ _ _ _ _ _

10. You form these to play football. ■ _ _ _ _ _

11. These are held on birthdays. ▲ _ _ _ _ _ _

12. You see these bright lights after thunder. ◆ _ _ _ _ _ _ _ of lightning

13. They teach people on sports teams. ★ _ _ _ _ _ _ _

14. You read this in a book. ● _ _ _ _ _

15. These are big happenings. ▲ _ _ _ _ _ _

16. You use this to talk to someone. ■ _ _ _ _ _

17. People store garden tools in these. ★ _ _ _ _

18. It comes after Thursday. ▲ _ _ _ _ _

19. People use these to hold items. ◆ _ _ _ _ _ _

20. You use these to chew food. ● _ _ _ _ _

wrap	feeling	crash	glasses	partly
level	meeting	agree	bother	belonged
returning	burn	rolled	greet	glow
hoping	laugh	sport	copy	grind

B. Bases and Endings

Write an Other Word Form for each base word. If you need help, use the **Spelling Dictionary**.

1. wrap

2. level

3. burn

4. laugh

5. crash

6. agree

7. sport

8. bother

9. greet

10. copy

11. glow

12. grind

Write the base word and one Other Word Form for each spelling word. If you need help, use the **Spelling Dictionary**.

Spelling Word	Base Word	Other Word Form
Example: returning	r e t u r n	*returned*
13. hoping		
14. feeling		
15. meeting		
16. rolled		
17. glasses		
18. partly		
19. belonged		

awoke	clever	lamb	real	stole
beef	eleven	nobody	saddle	sure
between	handle	paddle	Saturday	turtle
cattle	jar	provide	seat	wrong
cheer	job	quiet	seventh	yard

C. Farmyard Foul-ups Write Other Word Forms or the spelling words to complete these scenes that you may or may not see at a farm. Write each word or its Other Word Form only once. If you need help, use the **Spelling Dictionary**.

1. ants stuck to __ __ __ __ of honey spilled in the two __ __ __ __ __
jar   yard

2. __ __ __ __ __ __ ducks __ __ __ __ __ __ __ __ backwards
seventh   paddle

3. shoes __ __ __ __ __ __ __ for horses but put on the __ __ __ __ __ feet
provide   wrong

4. children __ __ __ __ __ __ __ chicks __ __ __ __ __ __ __
handle   quiet

5. baby __ __ __ __ __ running __ __ __ __ __ __ __ mother's legs
lamb   between

6. cooks __ __ __ __ __ __ __ spicing the __ __ __ __ for the noon meal
clever   beef

7. __ __ __ __ __ __ dirty pigs that __ __ __ __ __ __ wants to be near
real   nobody

8. children __ __ __ __ __ __ __ for the __ __ __ __ __ __ __ in the race
cheer   turtle

9. no __ __ __ __ __ for __ __ __ __ __ __ hens to hatch their eggs
seat   eleven

10. __ __ __ __ __ __ being __ __ __ __ __ __ for horses' __ __ __ __
cattle   saddle   job

11. a fox __ __ __ __ __ __ planning to return the __ __ __ __ __ __ __ eggs
sure   stole

12. roosters __ __ __ __ __ __ early on a __ __ __ __ __ __ __ __ __
awoke   Saturday

alone	crack	harm	remind	steep
battle	drank	heel	shore	strong
chop	fled	indeed	smoke	tear
chose	fond	led	sob	tiny
coal	golden	monster	spoke	ton

D. Break the Code Use the code to write an Other Word Form or a spelling word.

1	2	3	4	5	6	7	8	9	10	11	12	13	14	15	16	17	18
↓	↓	↓	↓	↓	↓	↓	↓	↓	↓	↓	↓	↓	↓	↓	↓	↓	↓
a	b	c	d	e	f	g	h	i	k	l	m	n	o	p	r	s	t

1. __ __ __ __ __ __ __
2 1 18 18 11 5 17

2. __ __ __ __ __
11 5 1 4 17

3. __ __ __ __ __ __
9 13 4 5 5 4

4. __ __ __ __ __ __ __ __
6 14 13 4 13 5 17 17

5. __ __ __ __
6 11 5 5

6. __ __ __ __ __ __ __ __
17 18 16 14 13 7 5 16

7. __ __ __ __ __
3 14 1 11 17

8. __ __ __ __ __ __ __
18 9 13 9 5 17 18

9. __ __ __ __ __ __ __
3 16 1 3 10 5 4

10. __ __ __ __ __ __ __ __
12 14 13 17 18 5 16 17

11. __ __ __ __ __ __ __
17 12 14 10 9 13 7

12. __ __ __ __
18 14 13 17

13. __ __ __ __ __ __ __
16 5 12 9 13 4 17

14. __ __ __ __ __
18 5 1 16 17

15. __ __ __ __ __ __
17 15 14 10 5 13

16. __ __ __ __ __
1 11 14 13 5

17. __ __ __ __ __ __ __
17 14 2 2 9 13 7

18. __ __ __ __
7 14 11 4

19. __ __ __ __ __ __
17 8 14 16 5 17

20. __ __ __ __ __ __
8 1 16 12 5 4

21. __ __ __ __ __
4 16 9 13 10

22. __ __ __ __ __ __
3 8 14 17 5 13

23. __ __ __ __ __ __ __
3 8 14 15 15 5 4

24. __ __ __ __ __ __ __ __
17 18 5 5 15 5 17 18

25. __ __ __ __ __
8 5 5 11 17

25

A. Pretest and Proofreading

B. Spelling Words and Phrases

1.	peek	to <u>peek</u> into the box
2.	queen	dressed like a <u>queen</u>
3.	sheet	a flowered <u>sheet</u>
4.	steel	<u>steel</u> rod
5.	wheel	behind the <u>wheel</u>
6.	sweep	to <u>sweep</u> into a pile
7.	sleepy	<u>sleepy</u> child
8.	flow	<u>flow</u> of the river
9.	slowly	crawled <u>slowly</u>
10.	throw	the longest <u>throw</u>
11.	grown	<u>grown</u> older
12.	shown	had <u>shown</u> me
13.	owner	found the <u>owner</u>
14.	hero	medal for the <u>hero</u>
15.	danger	sign of <u>danger</u>
16.	ranger	the <u>ranger</u> on duty
17.	strange	a <u>strange</u> sound
18.	change	too much <u>change</u>
19.	chance	not a <u>chance</u>
20.	dancing	<u>dancing</u> in a circle

Other Word Forms

peeked, peeking
queens, queenly
sheets
steels, steely
wheels, wheeled
swept, sweeping
sleep, sleeps, slept,
  sleepier, sleepiest
flows, flowed
slow, slowed, slower,
  slowest
threw, thrown

grow, grows, grew, growing
show, shows, showing
own, owns, owners
heroes
dangerous
range, ranges, ranged,
  ranging
stranger, strangest, strangely
changed, changing,
  changeable
chances
dance, dances

C. Visual Warm-up

Write the spelling word for each shape.

a.
b.
c.
d.
e.
f.
g.
h.
i.
j.
k.
l.
m.
n.
o.
p.
q.
r.
s.
t.

D. Three in a Row Write a spelling word for the group it best fits.

1. prince, king, _____
2. odd, weird, _____
3. tired, drowsy, _____
4. walking, skipping, _____
5. look, stare, _____
6. iron, brass, _____
7. buyer, seller, _____
8. shovel, rake, _____
9. catch, pitch, _____
10. blanket, towel, _____
11. harm, trouble, _____
12. winner, champion, _____

E. Scrambled Words Unscramble each scrambled word to find the spelling word that completes the sentence. Write the word.

1. We watched the gentle _____ (wofl) of the stream.
2. The bud had _____ (wnogr) into a flower.
3. We drove _____ (lslwoy) on the icy road.
4. The team had no _____ (acench) of winning.
5. The guide had _____ (ownsh) us the way.
6. Put a new _____ (elewh) on this bike.
7. Will you _____ (ngeach) the tire?
8. The forest _____ (ngrear) is in the tower.

Spelling Words

peek	*queen*	*sheet*	*steel*	*wheel*
sweep	*sleepy*	*flow*	*slowly*	*throw*
grown	*shown*	*owner*	*hero*	*danger*
ranger	*strange*	*change*	*chance*	*dancing*

F. Bases and Suffixes The spelling list contains thirteen base words and seven words with suffixes. Write each spelling word.

Words with Suffixes	Base Words		Words with Suffixes	Base Words
1. sweeping	____		**11.** wheeled	____
2. steely	____		**12.** peeking	____
3. heroes	____		**13.** dangerous	____
4. strangely	____		**14.** ____	slow
5. flowed	____		**15.** ____	range
6. changeable	____		**16.** ____	grow
7. queenly	____		**17.** ____	show
8. chances	____		**18.** ____	sleep
9. sheets	____		**19.** ____	dance
10. thrown	____		**20.** ____	own

G. Using Other Word Forms
Write the Other Word Form that fits each group of words.

Base Words: throw(ew)   sleepy(er)   hero(es)   change(ing)   strange(ly)

1. good guys, idols, superstars, _____

2. tossed, flung, passed, _____

3. unusually, oddly, weirdly, _____

4. replacing, swapping, switching, _____

5. more tired, drowsier, more exhausted, _____

H. Challenge Words
Write the Challenge Word that fits each clue.

vocabulary	deepest	detail	potato	measles

1. can be mashed or fried

2. like mumps or chicken pox

3. a lot of words

4. not at all shallow

5. a fine point

I. Spelling and Writing
Write *two* or more answers to each question. Use as many Spelling Words, Other Word Forms, and Challenge Words as you can. A few words are suggested. Proofread your work.

1. What would you do to make sure that you did not get lost if you were hiking in a park or a forest?

danger – ranger – change – detail

2. What would you do if you couldn't find your pet cat?

peek – sheet – sleepy – shown – owner

3. What would you do if you walked into your house and found water leaking everywhere?

sweep – flow – slowly – strange – deepest

26

A. Pretest and Proofreading

B. Spelling Words and Phrases

1.	shape	triangular shape
2.	hate	hate to be late
3.	lately	not lately
4.	making	making lunch
5.	lazy	felt very lazy
6.	sharing	sharing their toys
7.	careful	careful on a bike
8.	careless	careless around tools
9.	February	since February
10.	tend	tend to wait too long
11.	less	much less
12.	lesson	next lesson
13.	letting	letting me sing
14.	friends	some of my friends
15.	field	a field of daisies
16.	apiece	had three apiece
17.	fried	box of fried clams
18.	cried	cried softly
19.	lying	was caught lying
20.	nineteen	nineteen minutes

Other Word Forms

shapes, shaping
hates, hated, hateful
late, later, latest
make, makes, made
lazier, laziest
share, shares, shared
care, cares, caring,
  carelessness
Feb.
tends, tended, tending
little, lesser, least, lessen

lessons
let, lets
friend, friendly,
  friendship
fields
fry, fries, frying
cry, cries, crying
lie, lies, lied, liar
nineteenth

C. Visual Warm-up

Write the spelling word for each shape.

a.

b.

c.

d.

e.

f.

g.

h.

i.

j.

k.

l.

m.

n.

o.

p.

q.

r.

s.

t.

D. All in a Row Write the twenty spelling words in alphabetical order. Then join the boxed letters and write four hidden words.

1. _ ☐ _ _ _ _

2. _ _ _ ☐ _ _ _

3. _ ☐ _ _ _ _ _ _

4. ☐ _ _ _ _ _

5. _ ☐ _ _ _ _ _ _

6. Hidden Word =

7. ☐ _ _ _ _ _

8. _ _ ☐ _ _

9. _ _ _ _ _ _ ☐

10. ☐ _ _ _

11. _ _ _ _ _ ☐

12. Hidden Word =

13. _ ☐ _ _

14. ☐ _ _ _ _

15. ☐ _ _ _ _ _ _

16. _ ☐ _ _ _ _ _ _

17. _ ☐ _ _ _

18. Hidden Word =

19. ☐ _ _ _ _ _ _

20. _ _ _ _ _ ☐ _ _

21. _ _ ☐ _ _

22. _ _ _ _ _ ☐ _

23. ☐ _ _ _

24. Hidden Word =

E. Word Opposites Antonyms are word opposites. Write the antonym from the spelling list for each word or words below.

1. enemies
2. more
3. love
4. busy
5. careless

6. truthful
7. laughed
8. careful
9. long ago

Spelling Words

shape	hate	lately	making	lazy
sharing	careful	careless	February	tend
less	lesson	letting	friends	field
apiece	fried	cried	lying	nineteen

F. Base Words The spelling list contains nine base words and eleven words that are not base words. Write each spelling word.

	Words That Are Not Base Words	Base Words		Words That Are Not Base Words	Base Words
1.	lessons	_____	**11.**	_____	lie
2.	fields	_____	**12.**	_____	friend
3.	shaping	_____	**13.**	_____	let
4.	nineteenth	_____	**14.**	_____	little
5.	tending	_____	**15.**	_____	care
6.	Feb.	_____	**16.**	_____	late
7.	laziest	_____	**17.**	_____	care
8.	hateful	_____	**18.**	_____	make
9.	_____	fry	**19.**	_____	share
10.	_____	cry			

20. Write the one base word not used above.

G. Using Other Word Forms Write the Other Word Form that completes each question.

Base Words: lazy(er) friend(ship) shape(ing) lie(ar) fry(ing)

1. He told a lie. Was he a _____?

2. They fried the potatoes. Did they use a _____ pan?

3. They were good pals. Did they have a good _____ ?

4. The dog was much more lazy. Was the dog _____ ?

5. She was forming a ball of clay. Was she _____ it with her hands?

H. Challenge Words Write the Challenge Word that completes each phrase.

petal	checkers	spices	text	wages

1. either chess or _____

2. either salary or _____

3. either seasoning or _____

4. either a flower part or a _____

5. either printed words or _____

I. Spelling and Writing Write *two* or more answers to each question. Use as many Spelling Words, Other Word Forms, and Challenge Words as you can. A few words are suggested. Proofread your work.

1. What would you do if you arrived at a party and found that you knew only one person?

careful – lesson – making – checkers

2. What would you think if you opened a beautifully wrapped birthday present and found that the box was empty?

tend – sharing – careless – lying

3. What would you think if your friend served you soup on the hottest day of the summer?

February – spices – lately – fried

A. Pretest and Proofreading

B. Spelling Words and Phrases

1.	cabin	cabin in the woods
2.	magic	a magic show
3.	habit	a good habit
4.	blast	blast of the rocket
5.	basket	threw it into the basket
6.	absent	never absent
7.	fence	painted the fence
8.	sense	makes lots of sense
9.	cents	forty-five cents
10.	center	open in the center
11.	December	December holiday
12.	plenty	plenty of time
13.	twenty	twenty miles to go
14.	twenty-five	twenty-five days
15.	ripe	almost ripe
16.	likely	likely to try again
17.	sidewalk	cement sidewalk
18.	sideways	sideways as a crab
19.	fireplace	in front of the fireplace
20.	tired	hot and tired

Other Word Forms

cabins	Dec.
magical, magically, magician	plentiful
habits	twentieth
blasts, blasting	twenty-fifth
baskets	ripen, ripening, riper, ripest
absently, absentee	like, likes, liked, liking
fences, fenced, fencing	sidewalks
senses, sensed, sensing, senseless	fireplace
cent	tire, tires, tiring, tiresome, tireless
centers, centered, centering	

C. Visual Warm-up
Write the spelling word for each shape.

a.
b.
c.
d.
e.
f.
g.
h.
i.
j.
k.
l.
m.
n.
o.
p.
q.
r.
s.
t.

D. Missing Vowels Find the missing vowels and write the spelling words.

1. s __ ns __
2. bl __ st
3. b __ sk __ t
4. h __ b __ t
5. f __ nc __
6. t __ r __ d
7. r __ p __
8. m __ g __ c
9. c __ nts
10. pl __ nt __

11. tw __ nt __
12. tw __ nt __ -f __ v __
13. c __ b __ n
14. c __ nt __ r
15. __ bs __ nt
16. l __ k __ l __
17. s __ d __ w __ __ s
18. D __ c __ mb __ r
19. f __ r __ pl __ c __
20. s __ d __ w __ lk

E. Anagrams Change the letters around in these words and write the spelling words.

1. scent ____
2. tried ____

3. pier ____

F. Compound Words Join the eight words to write four compound words.

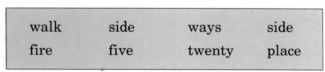

| walk | side | ways | side |
| fire | five | twenty | place |

Spelling Words

cabin	magic	habit	blast	basket
absent	fence	sense	cents	center
December	plenty	twenty	twenty-five	ripe
likely	sidewalks	sideways	fireplace	tired

G. Sound-alikes Write the two homophones from the spelling list.

H. Words and Meanings Write a spelling word for each meaning. Check your answers in the **Spelling Dictionary**.

1. a small, plain house
2. the twelfth month of the year
3. completely grown and ready for eating
4. a wall that protects an area
5. good judgment
6. done by using tricks
7. not present
8. a full supply of all that's needed
9. an explosion, or loud noise
10. a place by the street where people can walk
11. an opening that holds a fire
12. a woven container
13. an action repeated over and over
14. half of fifty
15. a few pennies
16. with one side facing forward
17. to be expected
18. the middle part of something
19. two times ten
20. weary, or worn out

I. Using Other Word Forms Write the Other Word Form that completes each sentence.

Base Words: absent(ee) plenty(ful) ripe(n) tire(ing) magic(ian)

1. The ____ made the coin disappear.
2. This hard work is ____ .
3. Water is ____ in the ocean.
4. The banana must ____ before you eat it.
5. The ____ had to bring a written excuse.

J. Challenge Words Write the Challenge Word that completes each word pair.

hamburger	cannon	retired	slender	tremble

1. rifle or ____
2. hot dog or ____
3. thin or ____
4. shiver or ____
5. resigned or ____

K. Spelling and Writing Write two or more answers to each question. Use as many Spelling Words, Other Word Forms, and Challenge Words as you can. A few words are suggested. Proofread for spelling using one of the Proofreading Tips from the Yellow Pages.

1. What do campers do at the end of the day?
   fireplace   tired   cabin   sensed   fence   hamburger
2. Where will the magician do his tricks?
   magic   sidewalk   twenty   likely   centered   tremble
3. How much candy did Rita sell?
   plentiful   twenty-five   basket   cents   habit   slender

28

A. Pretest and Proofreading

B. Spelling Words and Phrases

1.	busy	should be <u>busy</u>
2.	build	would like to <u>build</u>
3.	built	<u>built</u> of bricks
4.	inch	just one more <u>inch</u>
5.	print	large, even <u>print</u>
6.	swing	high on the <u>swing</u>
7.	living	<u>living</u> next door
8.	aid	came to our <u>aid</u>
9.	afraid	<u>afraid</u> to enter
10.	chain	<u>chain</u> on the gate
11.	drain	will <u>drain</u> the water
12.	rainy	something for a <u>rainy</u> day
13.	mailed	<u>mailed</u> the letter
14.	waiting	<u>waiting</u> for the bus
15.	repair	will <u>repair</u> it soon
16.	oak	an <u>oak</u> table
17.	loads	<u>loads</u> of lumber
18.	roar	the <u>roar</u> of water
19.	board	balanced on the <u>board</u>
20.	floor	waxed the <u>floor</u>

Other Word Forms

busier, busiest	mail, mails, mailing
builds, building, builder	wait, waits, waited,
inches, inched	waiter, waitress
prints, printing, printer	repairs, repaired,
swings, swinging, swung	repairing
live, lived	oaks
aids, aided, aiding	load, loaded, loading
chains, chained, chaining	roars, roared, roaring
drains, draining	boards, boarded,
rain, rained, raining,	boarding, boarder
rainier, rainiest	floors

C. Visual Warm-up

Write the spelling word for each shape.

a.

b.

c.

d.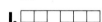

e.

f.

g.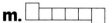

h.

i.

j.

k.

l.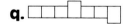

m.

n.

o.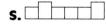

p.

q.

r.

s.

t.

D. Sort Your Words Write each spelling word in the correct column. Two words go in more than one column. Check your answers in the **Spelling Dictionary**.

Words with *ai*	Words with *oa*	Words with a Short *i* Sound
1. ____	9. ____	13. ____
2. ____	10. ____	14. ____
3. ____	11. ____	15. ____
4. ____	12. ____	16. ____
5. ____		17. ____
6. ____		18. ____
7. ____		19. ____
8. ____		20. ____
		21. ____

22. Write the word that did not fit in any column. ____

E. Base Words The spelling list contains fourteen base words and six words that are not base words. Write each spelling word.

Words That Are Not Base Words	Base Words	Words That Are Not Base Words	Base Words
1. oaks	____	11. boarded	____
2. chains	____	12. inched	____
3. building	____	13. roaring	____
4. busiest	____	14. ____	live
5. repaired	____	15. ____	wait
6. drains	____	16. ____	mail
7. swinging	____	17. ____	load
8. aided	____	18. ____	build
9. floors	____	19. ____	rain
10. printer	____		

20. Write the one base word not used above.

Spelling Words

busy	build	built	inch	print	swing
living	aid	afraid	chain	drain	rainy
mailed	waiting	repair	oak	loads	roar
board	floor				

F. Unscramble and Write Unscramble each scrambled word to find the spelling word that completes the sentence. Write the word.

1. I heard the _____ (oarr) of the lion.
2. Did you _____ (pearri) the broken wheel?
3. I'm not _____ (daifra) of the dark.
4. Every _____ (naich) has links.
5. I will _____ (aindr) the soapy water.
6. My cousin _____ (laimed) the letter.
7. Bees are _____ (suby) insects.
8. Did you _____ (lduib) a snow fort?
9. We must _____ (ntpir) our names.
10. They carried many _____ (doals) of books.
11. Today is a _____ (niray) day.
12. No _____ (dia) is needed to finish the job.
13. The house was _____ (ltibu) in 1860.
14. The _____ (ngisw) needs a new seat.
15. There are elm and _____ (koa) trees in our yard.
16. We are _____ (angwiti) for a friend.
17. An _____ (chni) is smaller than a foot.
18. One oak _____ (bardo) is all we need.
19. A wool rug covers the _____ (roflo).
20. My sister is _____ (ingvil) in Texas.

G. Using Other Word Forms Write the Other Word Form that completes each sentence.

Base Words: rainy(er) board(ing) wait(r)(ess) busy(est) repair(ed)

1. No one was as busy as my brother. He was the ____ .

2. It rained more today than yesterday. Today is ____ .

3. She served our meal. She was our ____ .

4. She fixed the bicycle. The bike is now ____ .

5. The pirates were coming onto the ship. They were ____ it.

H. Challenge Words Write the Challenge Word that completes each sentence.

cardboard	thrilling	distance	erase	therefore

1. We traveled a long ____ .

2. Use heavy paper or ____ .

3. I'm your friend; ____ , you can count on me.

4. The roller coaster is a ____ ride.

5. I'll ____ the chalkboard.

I. Spelling and Writing Write *two* or more answers to each question. Use as many Spelling Words, Other Word Forms, and Challenge Words as you can. A few words are suggested. Proofread your work.

1. What would you do if your tree house was ruined in a bad wind storm?
busy – build – repair – board – oak

2. What would you do if you were the only survivor after a shipwreck?
afraid – rainy – living – aid – thrilling

3. What would you want to know before entering a poster-drawing contest?
print – inch – mailed – erase – cardboard

29

A. Pretest and Proofreading

B. Spelling Words and Phrases

1. sack — sack of potatoes
2. cash — to cash a check
3. mask — a plain black mask
4. gang — tried to gang up
5. demand — to demand a reply
6. grandmother — grandmother and aunt
7. basketball — a game of basketball
8. none — but there were none
9. front — through the front door
10. above — above them all
11. month — one month later
12. Monday — on a rainy Monday
13. honey — honey from the hive
14. discover — tried to discover
15. recover — will recover my breath
16. thousand — a thousand times
17. amount — very small amount
18. around — around the next corner
19. bound — bound with rope
20. wound — wound around their legs

Other Word Forms

sacks	honeys, honeyed
cashes, cashed, cashing, cashier	discovers, discovered, discovering, discoverer, discovery
masks, masked, masking	recovers, recovered, recovering, recovery
gangs	thousands, thousandth
demands, demanded, demanding	amounts, amounted, amounting
grandmothers	bind, binds, binding
basketballs	wind, winding
front	
months, monthly	
Mon.	

C. Visual Warm-up

Write the spelling word for each shape.

a.
b.
c.
d.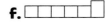
e.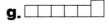
f.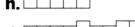
g.
h.
i.
j.
k.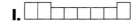
l.
m.
n.
o.
p.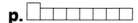
q.
r.
s.
t.

D. Sort Your Words

1. Write the seven words with a short *a* sound. Check your answers in the **Spelling Dictionary**. Circle the two letters that follow the letter that spells the short *a* sound.

2. Write the nine words with a short *u* sound.

3. What letter spells the short *u* sound?

4. Write the five words with the *ou* sound as in *ouch*. Circle the word that could also have the *oo* sound as in *boot*.

5. Write the two compound words.

E. Not This, but That Write spelling words to complete the phrases below.

1. not a check, but _____

2. not Sunday, but _____

3. not below, but _____

4. not between, but _____

5. not a costume, but a _____

6. not grandfather, but _____

7. not a basket, but a _____

8. not many, but _____

9. not hundred, but _____

10. not back, but _____

11. not ask, but _____

12. not sugar, but _____

13. not one, but a _____

14. not year, but _____

15. not a part, but an _____

16. not hide, but _____

17. not baseball, but _____

18. not lose, but _____

19. not untied, but _____

20. not unwound, but _____

Spelling Words

sack	cash	mask	gang	demand
grandmother	basketball	none	front	above
month	Monday	honey	discover	recover
thousand	amount	around	bound	wound

F. Crossword Puzzle Solve the puzzle by using words from the spelling list. Write the words. Check your answers in the **Spelling Dictionary**.

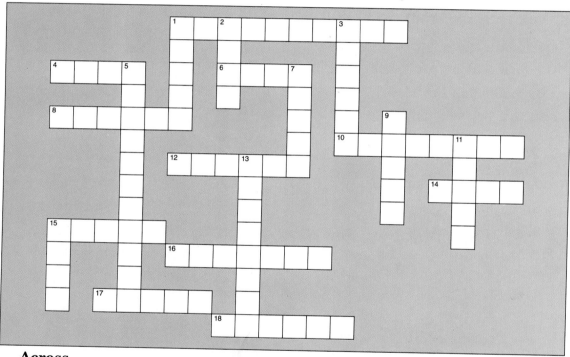

Across
1. a sport played on a court
4. a large group
6. money
8. to ask for strongly
10. ten times one hundred
12. a day of the week
14. not any
15. part of a year
16. to get back something lost
17. the part facing forward
18. in a circle

Down
1. tied
2. a bag
3. the total
5. your father's mother
7. a liquid made by bees
9. wrapped around
11. not below
13. to find out for the first time
15. a face covering

G. Using Other Word Forms Write the Other Word Form that answers each question.

Base Words: thousand(th) recover(y) discover(y) cash(ier) month(ly)

1. Who collects the money at the store?

2. How often does the calendar need to be changed?

3. What follows the nine hundred ninety-ninth?

4. What did Christopher Columbus hope to make?

5. What does a hospital patient hope to make?

H. Challenge Words Write the Challenge Word that completes each word pair.

couches	crumbled	cloudy	halves	shoved

1. shattered and _____

2. rainy and _____

3. wholes and _____

4. pushed and _____

5. sofas and _____

Level D – p.119

I. Spelling and Writing Write two or more questions about each statement. Use as many Spelling Words, Other Word Forms, and Challenge Words as you can. A few words are suggested. Proofread for spelling using one of the Proofreading Tips from the Yellow Pages.

1. Some people shop once a week.
sack cash month Monday honey front amount crumbled

Example: Did you find <u>honey</u> at the <u>front</u> or the back of the market?

2. Fifty years ago the town was very different.
around grandmother discovered wound thousand above

3. The story was about an unsuccessful robbery.
mask gang demanding recovered bound none shoved

30

☐ grown	☆ cried	▲ dancing	◆ bound	● lesson
field	cents	friends	basket	fireplace
build	loads	wound	rainy	mailed
honey	waiting	above	gang	grandmother
throw	month	fried	lazy	afraid

A. Words in a Series Use Other Word Forms or the spelling words to complete each series. The shapes tell you in what column you can find the spelling word. Write each word or its Other Word Form only once.

1. groups, crowds, ◆ _ _ _ _ _

2. moves, steps, ▲ _ _ _ _ _ _

3. bees, sweetener, ☐ _ _ _ _ _

4. days, weeks, ☆ _ _ _ _ _ _

5. shower, sprinkle, ◆ _ _ _ _ _

6. pal, person, ▲ _ _ _ _ _ _

7. pastures, meadows, ☐ _ _ _ _ _ _

8. sobbing, weeping, ☆ _ _ _ _ _

9. stayed, rested, ☆ _ _ _ _ _ _

10. buckets, boxes, ◆ _ _ _ _ _ _

11. making, stacking, ☐ _ _ _ _ _ _ _

12. cooking, browning, ▲ _ _ _ _ _

13. frightened, scared, ● _ _ _ _ _

14. filling, packing, ☆ _ _ _ _ _ _

15. assignments, exercises, ● _ _ _ _ _ _

16. becoming, raising, ☐ _ _ _ _ _ _

17. overhead, higher, ▲ _ _ _ _ _

18. tossing, pitching, ☐ _ _ _ _ _

19. chimneys, hearths, ● _ _ _ _ _ _ _ _

20. person, relative, ● _ _ _ _ _ _ _ _ _

21. tied, knotted, ◆ _ _ _ _ _

22. penny, coin, ☆ _ _ _ _ _

23. wrap, coil, ▲ _ _ _ _

24. tired, slow, ◆ _ _ _ _

25. send, postmark, ● _ _ _ _ _

absent	December	letting	plenty	sideways
busy	February	likely	ranger	steel
careful	front	Monday	ripe	strange
careless	hero	none	sack	sweep
danger	less	owner	sidewalk	tired

B. Bag of Words Find the missing letters and write the Other Word Forms. If you need help, use the **Spelling Dictionary**.

The *s* Bag

1. s __ __ __ __ s
2. o __ __ __ __ s
3. r __ __ __ __ __ s
4. d __ __ __ __ __ s
5. l __ __ s
6. s __ __ __ __ __ __ s
7. t __ __ __ s
8. l __ __ __ s
9. f __ __ __ __ s
10. s __ __ __ s
11. s __ __ __ __ s

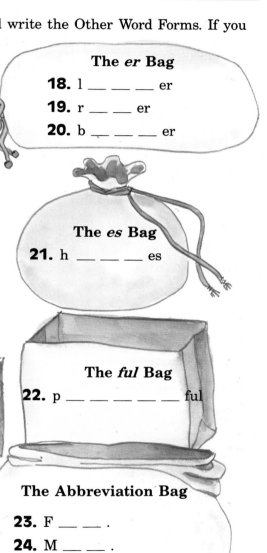

The *er* Bag

18. l __ __ __ er
19. r __ __ er
20. b __ __ __ er

The *es* Bag

21. h __ __ __ __ es

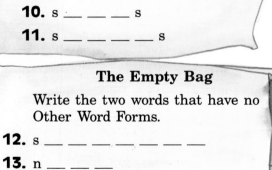

The Empty Bag

Write the two words that have no Other Word Forms.

12. s __ __ __ __ __ __ __
13. n __ __ __

The *ful* Bag

22. p __ __ __ __ __ __ ful

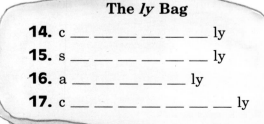

The *ly* Bag

14. c __ __ __ __ __ __ ly
15. s __ __ __ __ __ __ __ ly
16. a __ __ __ __ __ ly
17. c __ __ __ __ __ __ __ ly

The Abbreviation Bag

23. F __ __ .
24. M __ __ .
25. D __ __ .

■ slowly	★ sharing	▲ drain	◆ twenty	● oak
sheet	making	nineteen	built	thousand
queen	lately	cabin	swing	around
sleepy	apiece	magic	floor	basketball
shown	lying	habit	living	twenty-five

C. What a Feeling!

Write Other Word Forms or the spelling words to complete these ideas that could make you feel good. The shapes tell you in what column you can find the spelling word. Write each word or its Other Word Form only once. If you need help, use the **Spelling Dictionary**.

1. playing ● _ _ _ _ _ _ _ _ _ _ on a warm spring day

2. pretending to be a ■ _ _ _ _ _ who ◆ _ _ _ _ _ in a castle

3. getting into a bed freshly ★ _ _ _ _ with clean ■ _ _ _ _ _

4. finding only ● _ _ _ _ _ _ _ - _ _ _ _ questions instead of one
   ● _ _ _ _ _ _ _ _ on your math test.

5. ◆ _ _ _ _ _ _ _ _ _ a fence ● _ _ _ _ _ _ your garden

6. smelling the pine ◆ _ _ _ _ _ _ in a summer ▲ _ _ _ _ _

7. ■ _ _ _ _ _ _ _ a ▲ _ _ _ _ _ trick and having it work

8. waking your ■ _ _ _ _ _ _ _ _ brother so he isn't
   ★ _ _ _ _ _ for school

9. selling your homemade bookmarks for ◆ _ _ _ _ _ _ cents
   ★ _ _ _ _ _ _ at the school fair

10. having ▲ _ _ _ _ _ _ _ _ _ cookies to ★ _ _ _ _ _ _

11. having your teacher say that your study ▲ _ _ _ _ _ _ have
   ■ _ _ _ _ _ _ improved

12. ◆ _ _ _ _ _ _ _ _ _ on a tire under the ● _ _ _ tree

13. finding out that your friend did not ★ _ _ _ _ to you

14. fixing the clogged ▲ _ _ _ _ _ in the kitchen sink

change	peek	center	aid	mask
hate	tend	roar	shape	repair
chance	blast	board	demand	recover
wheel	sense	chain	amount	print
flow	fence	inch	cash	discover

D. Word Building Add word parts to each spelling word to make Other Word Forms. The dots indicate which word parts to add. Write the words.

Spelling Words	*s* or *es*	*ed*	*ing*
Example: walk	*walks*	*walked*	*walking*
1. blast	●	●	●
2. chain	●	●	●
3. hate	●	●	●
4. peek	●	●	●
5. aid	●	●	●
6. print	●	●	●
7. change	●	●	●
8. fence	●	●	●
9. demand	●	●	●
10. mask	●	●	●
11. tend	●	●	●
12. center	●	●	●
13. amount	●	●	●
14. repair	●	●	●
15. wheel	●	●	●
16. sense	●	●	●
17. inch	●	●	●
18. shape	●	●	●
19. recover	●	●	●
20. flow	●	●	●
21. roar	●	●	●
22. cash	●	●	●
23. board	●	●	●
24. chance	●	●	●
25. discover	●	●	●

A. Pretest and Proofreading

B. Spelling Words and Phrases

1.	pool	jumped into the pool
2.	loop	loop in the rope
3.	root	root of the plant
4.	tooth	chipped a front tooth
5.	bloom	will bloom in spring
6.	speak	when you speak
7.	dream	unusual dream
8.	feast	the holiday feast
9.	beast	beast in the jungle
10.	cable	a new cable car
11.	stable	cleaning the stable
12.	paste	wallpaper paste
13.	waste	threw away the waste
14.	attic	in the dusty attic
15.	address	new address
16.	happening	happening to me
17.	sitting	sitting very straight
18.	bigger	not much bigger
19.	pillow	fluffed up the pillow
20.	middle	middle of the night

Other Word Forms

pools
loops, looped, looping
roots, rooted, rooting
teeth, toothy
blooms, bloomed, blooming
speaks, spoke, spoken,
 speaking
dreams, dreamed,
 dreaming, dreamer,
 dreamt
feasts, feasted, feasting
beasts, beastly

cables, cabled
stables, stabled
pastes, pasted, pasting
wastes, wasted, wasting,
 wasteful
attics
addresses, addressed
happen, happens,
 happened
sit, sits, sat
big, biggest
pillows

C. Visual Warm-up

Write the spelling word for each shape.

a.
b.
c.
d.
e.
f.
g.
h.
i.
j.
k.
l.
m.
n.
o.
p.
q.
r.
s.
t.

D. Sort Your Words In alphabetical order, write the spelling words where they belong.

Words with
Double Consonants

1. ____
2. ____
3. ____
4. ____
5. ____
6. ____
7. ____

Words with
Double Vowels

12. ____
13. ____
14. ____
15. ____
16. ____

Words with a
Long *a* Sound

8. ____
9. ____
10. ____
11. ____

Words with a
Long *e* Sound

17. ____
18. ____
19. ____
20. ____

E. Word Relatives Write the word from the spelling list that is related to each word or words below.

1. garbage
2. animal
3. nightmare
4. street
5. ribbon
6. flower
7. talk
8. taking place
9. bed
10. carrot

11. chew
12. top floor
13. center
14. chair
15. glue
16. meal
17. larger
18. barn
19. swimming
20. rope

Spelling Words

pool	loop	root	tooth	bloom
speak	dream	feast	beast	cable
stable	paste	waste	attic	address
happening	sitting	bigger	pillow	middle

F. Guide Words These word pairs are guide words that might appear in a dictionary. Write the words from the spelling list that would appear on the same page as each pair of guide words.

above – ax
1. _____   **2.** _____

backward – blade
3. _____   **4.** _____

blame – bucket
5. _____

build – change
6. _____

dirty – evening
7. _____

event – flock
8. _____

get – hate
9. _____

leaf – lucky
10. _____

mean – nineteen
11. _____

outfits – plum
12. _____   **13.** _____

pocket – purse
14. _____

returning – saves
15. _____

shell – sitting
16. _____

sob – straw
17. _____   **18.** _____

throw – unlock
19. _____

until – worry
20. _____

G. Using Other Word Forms Write the Other Word Form that fits each series.

Base Words: paste(ing) dream(ed) waste(ing) root(ed) feast(ing)

1. feasts, feasted, _____

2. pastes, pasted, _____

3. wastes, wasted, _____

4. dreams, _____, dreaming

5. roots, _____, rooting

H. Challenge Words Write the Challenge Word that fits each group of words.

juice	canteen	abandon	salmon	visiting

1. spawn, swim upstream, fish, _____

2. camping, water, container, _____

3. guests, drop in, calling on, _____

4. leave behind, give up, leave alone, _____

5. orange, breakfast, liquid, _____

I. Spelling and Writing Use each phrase in a sentence. You may want to use the words in a different order or use Other Word Forms. Proofread for spelling using one of the Proofreading Tips from the Yellow Pages.

1. pool our ideas

2. will root in soil

3. tooth of the saw

4. flowers in bloom

5. speak the language

6. dream of a lifetime

7. wild beast

8. cable television

9. paste together

10. waste no time

11. attic rooms

12. address the nation

13. an awesome happening

14. sitting on eggs

15. bigger than life

16. the middle ear

32

A. Pretest and Proofreading

B. Spelling Words and Phrases

1.	color	a bright color
2.	among	among their friends
3.	another	to one another
4.	anybody	if anybody knows
5.	follow	tried to follow
6.	gotten	had gotten lost
7.	October	cool October day
8.	orange	peeled the orange
9.	beat	a beat of the drum
10.	means	whatever it means
11.	reader	the next reader
12.	season	in any season
13.	leaving	leaving shortly
14.	nearest	to the nearest phone
15.	ray	a ray of sunshine
16.	May	in the month of May
17.	playmate	with my playmate
18.	always	always smiling
19.	sank	sank into the sea
20.	fallen	a fallen apple

Other Word Forms

colors, coloring	read, reads, reading
amongst	seasons, seasonal
follows, followed,	leave, leaves, left
following, follower	near, nearer, nearly
get, gets, got, getting	rays
Oct.	playmates
oranges	sink, sinks, sunk,
beats, beaten, beating	sinking
mean, meant, meaning	fall, falls, fell, falling

C. Visual Warm-up

Write the spelling word for each shape.

a.

b.

c.

d.

e.

f.

g.

h.

i.

j.

k.

l.

m.

n.

o.

p.

q.

r.

s.

t.

D. Missing Vowels Find the missing vowels and write the spelling words.

1. g __ tt __ n
2. m __ __ ns
3. f __ ll __ w
4. c __ l __ r
5. r __ __
6. __ m __ ng
7. s __ nk
8. f __ ll __ n
9. b __ __ t
10. M __ __

11. __ r __ ng __
12. __ lw __ __ s
13. __ ct __ b __ r
14. r __ __ d __ r
15. n __ __ r __ st
16. pl __ __ m __ t __
17. __ n __ th __ r
18. __ n __ b __ d __
19. l __ __ v __ ng
20. s __ __ s __ n

E. Hideaway Words from the spelling list are hiding in the underlined words in each sentence. Write the words.

1. Spring and (fall en)tice many tourists to the mountains. _____*fallen*_____
2. Can you display material for the sale?
3. The captain sailed the seas on a ship.
4. Bankers dread errors being made in money matters.
5. The tube attached to the beaker is broken.
6. The skater's ankle was swollen
7. The boss knows several ways to solve problems.
8. The farmer fears no ranges will be left for cattle.
9. The extra yam must be eaten.
10. He turns on that spigot ten times a day.
11. That dog is a mongrel.
12. Please give me answers to the questions.
13. Walk by the sea not here by the dunes.
14. Gone are stories of the wild West.

Spelling Words

color	among	another	anybody	follow
gotten	October	orange	beat	means
reader	season	leaving	nearest	ray
May	playmate	always	sank	fallen

F. Base Words The spelling list contains thirteen base words and seven words that are not base words. Write each spelling word.

Words That Are Not Base Words	Base Words		Words That Are Not Base Words	Base Words
1. coloring	_____	**9.**	_____	fall
2. rays	_____	**10.**	_____	sink
3. seasonal	_____	**11.**	_____	mean
4. follower	_____	**12.**	_____	near
5. beaten	_____	**13.**	_____	read
6. Oct.	_____	**14.**	_____	get
7. playmates	_____	**15.**	_____	leave
8. oranges	_____			

16. Write the five words not used above.

G. Using Other Word Forms Write the Other Word Form that completes each sentence.

Base Words: beat(en) near(ly) season(al) follow(ing) mean(t)

1. It was almost twelve o'clock. It was ____ noon.

2. He was behind her. He was ____ her.

3. The eggs and milk were mixed together. They were ____ .

4. He was serious about what he said. He really ____ it.

5. It happens every spring. It is a ____ celebration.

H. Challenge Words Write the Challenge Word that completes each sentence.

raiders	country	hauled	pioneers	beneath

1. If they're not colonists, they may be ____ .

2. If they're not on top, they may be ____ .

3. If they're not invaders, they may be ____ .

4. If it's not a continent, it may be a ____ .

5. If it's not carried, it may be ____ .

I. Spelling and Writing Write each set of words in a sentence. You may use Other Word Forms. Proofread your work.

1. May – October

2. playmate – leaving

3. always – gotten

4. ray – color

5. another – reader

6. anybody – means

7. season – follow

8. orange – fallen

9. among – beat

10. nearest – sank

11. country – pioneers

12. hauled – beneath

13. raiders – followed

A. Pretest and Proofreading

B. Spelling Words and Phrases

1.	born	born nine years ago
2.	fork	fork of the tree
3.	fort	built a snow fort
4.	forty	forty winks
5.	corner	piled in the corner
6.	before	before you're through
7.	fourth	the fourth grade
8.	fourteen	fourteen years old
9.	pouring	pouring from the pitcher
10.	silk	made of silk
11.	sink	dishes in the sink
12.	kick	a long, hard kick
13.	rich	a rich person
14.	film	watched the film
15.	windy	high on a windy hill
16.	enjoy	for you to enjoy
17.	second	in just one second
18.	pretend	when they pretend
19.	correct	correct time
20.	baseball	baseball cards

Other Word Forms

forks, forked
forts
fortieth
corners, cornered, cornering
four
fourteenth
pour, pours, poured
silky, silken
sinks, sinking, sank, sunk, sunken
kicks, kicked, kicking

richer, richest, richly
films, filmed, filming
wind, windier, windiest
enjoys, enjoyed, enjoying
seconds, seconded, seconding
pretends, pretending, pretended, pretender
corrects, corrected, correcting
baseballs

C. Visual Warm-up

Write the spelling word for each shape.

a.
b.
c.
d.
e.
f.
g.
h.
i.
j.
k.
l.
m.
n.
o.
p.
q.
r.
s.
t.

D. Sort Your Words In alphabetical order, write the spelling words under the correct headings. One word goes under two headings.

Words with *or* or *our*		Words in Which *i* Is Followed by Two Consonants		
1. ___	6. ___	11. ___	14. ___	16. ___
2. ___	7. ___	12. ___	15. ___	17. ___
3. ___	8. ___	13. ___		
4. ___	9. ___			
5. ___	10. ___			

18. Write the one compound word.

19. Write the three spelling words you have not used.

E. Three in a Row Write a spelling word for the group it best fits.

1. edge, end, ___

2. velvet, satin, ___

3. ___ , during, after

4. knife, spoon, ___

5. serving, flowing, ___

6. stormy, rainy, ___

7. stove, refrigerator, ___

8. make-believe, fake, ___

9. football, basketball, ___

10. cartoon, movie, ___

11. life, baby, ___

12. ___ , fifty, sixty

13. love, like, ___

14. second, third, ___

15. money, wealthy, ___

16. ___ , fifteen, sixteen

17. building, castle, ___

18. run, pass, ___

19. first, ___ , third

20. OK, right, ___

Spelling Words

born	fork	fort	forty	corner	before
fourth	fourteen	pouring	silk	sink	kick
rich	film	windy	enjoy	second	pretend
correct	baseball				

F. Guide Words These word pairs are guide words that might appear in a dictionary. Write the words from the spelling list that would appear on the same page as each pair of guide words.

backward – blade
1. _____   2. _____

blame – bucket
3. _____

chart – corner
4. _____

correct – dirty
5. _____

dirty – evening
6. _____

event – flock
7. _____

floor – gang
8. _____   11. _____
9. _____   12. _____
10. _____

kick – leading
13. _____

pocket – purse
14. _____   15. _____

returning – saves
16. _____

scale – sheet
17. _____

shell – sitting
18. _____   19. _____

until – worry
20. _____

G. Using Other Word Forms Write the Other Word Form that answers each question.

Base Words: fourteen(th) rich(est) silk(y) forty(eth) pretend(ing)

1. What comes after the thirty-ninth? the _____

2. Who is the person with the most money? the _____

3. How did the new dress feel? _____

4. What is the faker doing? _____

5. What date followed the thirteenth? the _____

H. Challenge Words Write the Challenge Word that completes each phrase.

adore	complain	rebels	orphans	kisses

1. not followers, but _____

2. not hugs, but _____

3. not agree, but _____

4. not dislike, but _____

5. not children with parents, but _____

I. Spelling and Writing Write two or more answers to each question. Use as many Spelling Words, Other Word Forms, and Challenge Words as you can. A few words are suggested. Proofread for spelling using one of the Proofreading Tips from the Yellow Pages.

1. How did the game end?
fourteenth   correct   before   baseball   windy   orphans

2. Where was the runaway horse caught?
corner   pretend   pouring   second   kicking   complain

3. What did the princess see at the party?
silk   rich   enjoying   film   forty   adore

34

A. Pretest and Proofreading

B. Spelling Words and Phrases

1. **huge** — a huge snowdrift
2. **June** — was finished last June
3. **July** — Fourth of July
4. **rules** — set of rules
5. **woman** — next to the woman
6. **ounce** — sold by the ounce
7. **pound** — 89¢ a pound
8. **count** — to count them again
9. **mouse** — signs of a mouse
10. **hour** — an hour ago
11. **flour** — ground into flour
12. **steam** — steam from the kettle
13. **stream** — rushing stream
14. **scream** — frightened scream
15. **sneakers** — brand-new sneakers
16. **inches** — measured in inches
17. **since** — since 1874
18. **picnic** — picnic basket
19. **picture** — hung the picture
20. **single** — in a single file

Other Word Forms

hugest, hugeness	steams, steamer
rule, ruled, ruling, ruler	streams
women, womanly	screams, screamed, screaming
ounces, oz.	sneaker
pounds, lb.	inch, inched, inching, in.
counts, counted, counting, counter	picnics, picnicking
mice	pictures, pictured, picturing
hours, hourly, hr.	singly
flours	

C. Visual Warm-up
Write the spelling word for each shape.

a.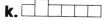

b.

c.

d.

e.

f.

g.

h.

i.

j.

k.

l.

m.

n.

o.

p.

q.

r.

s.

t.

D. Sort Your Words

1. Find the missing letters to make spelling words. Write the words.

    a. mou __ __

    b. __ __ ou __

    c. pou __ __

    d. ou __ __ __

    e. __ ou __

    f. cou __ __

    g. How are all these words alike?

2. Find the missing letters to make spelling words. Write the words.

    a. __ t __ ea __

    b. __ __ rea __

    c. __ __ ea __ __ __ __

    d. __ __ ea __

3. Write the five spelling words that have a short *i* sound.

4. Write the five spelling words you did not write above.

E. For Short Write the spelling word or Other Word Form (p. 136) for each abbreviation.

    1. hr.   **3.** lb.

    2. oz.   **4.** in.

Spelling Words

huge	June	July	rules	woman	ounce
pound	count	mouse	hour	flour	steam
stream	scream	sneakers	inches	since	picnic
picture	single				

F. Solve the Puzzle Solve the puzzle by using words from the spelling list. Write the words. Check your answers in the **Spelling Dictionary**.

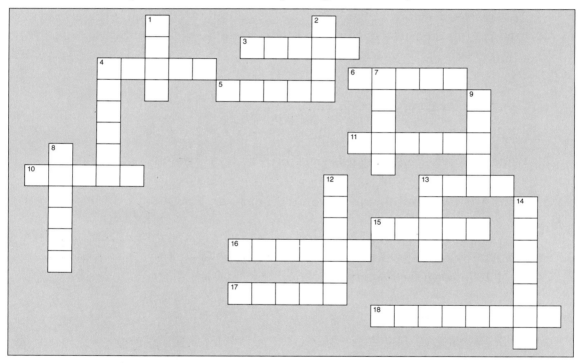

Across
3. used in baking
4. sixteen ounces
5. a small animal
6. to add up
10. from that time
11. a loud cry
13. the sixth month

15. laws
16. twelve in a foot
17. hot mist
18. gym shoes

Down
1. sixty minutes
2. large

4. an outdoor meal
7. a measure of weight
8. one
9. an adult female
12. a brook
13. the seventh month
14. a drawing

G. Using Other Word Forms Add an ending to each word to write an Other Word Form.

Base Words: picture(ing) picnic(ing) scream(ing) count(ing) rule(ing)

1. rule + ing = _____

2. scream + ing = _____

3. count + ing = _____

4. picture + ing = _____

5. picnic + ing = _____

H. Challenge Words Write the Challenge Word that completes each sentence.

indent	butcher	beetle	believe	scooped

1. Once I was a meat packer; now I'm a _____ .

2. Once I saw an ant; now I see a _____ .

3. Once I doubted you; now I _____ you.

4. Once I wrote beside the margin; now I _____ each paragraph.

5. Once the sherbet was spooned; now it is _____ .

I. Spelling and Writing Use each phrase in a sentence. You may want to use the words in a different order or use Other Word Forms. Proofread for spelling using one of the Proofreading Tips from the Yellow Pages.

1. <u>huge</u> buildings

2. one <u>June</u> day

3. a week in <u>July</u>

4. the <u>woman</u> I know

5. weighs an <u>ounce</u>

6. <u>count</u> each person

7. each working <u>hour</u>

8. <u>flour</u> for bread

9. <u>steam</u> heat

10. running <u>stream</u>

11. <u>scream</u> for joy

12. twelve <u>inches</u>

13. <u>since</u> you left

14. summer <u>picnic</u>

15. moving <u>picture</u>

16. in a <u>single</u> room

35

A. Pretest and Proofreading

B. Spelling Words and Phrases

1.	omit	if you <u>omit</u> two words
2.	only	the <u>only</u> one left
3.	ocean	swam in the <u>ocean</u>
4.	opening	through the <u>opening</u>
5.	poem	a twelve-line <u>poem</u>
6.	hotel	staying at the <u>hotel</u>
7.	clothes	changed my <u>clothes</u>
8.	clothing	<u>clothing</u> store
9.	dash	fifty-yard <u>dash</u>
10.	ranch	a large <u>ranch</u> house
11.	branch	local <u>branch</u> of the library
12.	handy	the <u>handy</u> tool kit
13.	packed	<u>packed</u> too tightly
14.	package	<u>package</u> of gum
15.	landing	stepped onto the <u>landing</u>
16.	evening	a summer <u>evening</u>
17.	fever	a high <u>fever</u>
18.	everyone	enough for <u>everyone</u>
19.	everybody	if <u>everybody</u> knew
20.	everything	mixed <u>everything</u> together

Other Word Forms

omits, omitted, omitting
oceans
open, opens, opened,
  opener
poems, poet, poetry
hotels
cloth, clothe, clothed
dashes, dashed, dashing
rancher, ranches

branches, branched,
  branching
handier, handiest,
  handily
pack, packs, packing
packages, packaged
land, lands, landings
evenings
feverish

C. Visual Warm-up

Write the spelling word for each shape.

a.
b.
c.
d.
e.
f.
g.
h.
i.
j.
k.
l.
m.
n.
o.
p.
q.
r.
s.
t.

D. Break the Code Use the code to write the spelling words.

a	b	c	d	e	f	g	h	i	j	k	l	m
↕	↕	↕	↕	↕	↕	↕	↕	↕	↕	↕	↕	↕
z	y	x	w	v	u	t	s	r	q	p	o	n

1. lxvzm
2. wzhs
3. kzxpztv
4. slgvo
5. xolgsrmt
6. lmob
7. lkvmrmt
8. uvevi
9. vevmrmt
10. ozmwrmt

11. veviblmv
12. klvn
13. xolgsvh
14. lnrg
15. vevibgsrmt
16. kzxpvw
17. szmwb
18. yizmxs
19. vevibylwb
20. izmxs

E. Word Search The spelling words can be found in the puzzle. The words appear across and down. Write the words.

Across

1.
2.
3.
4.
5.
6.
7.
8.
9.
10.
11.

Down

12.
13.
14.
15.
16.
17.
18.
19.
20.

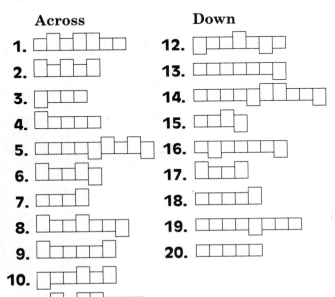

```
p c l o t h e s o v e
a h o t e l v n n e v
c c e s p o e m l r e
k s f e v e r o y u r
a a e v e r y b o d y
g y t e h o t r p a o
e h a n d y h g e s n
h o m i t n i t n h e
v l a n d i n g i r o
e s t g m e g p n a c
b r a n c h w z g n e
f p a c k e d r b c a
c l o t h i n g p h n
```

Spelling Words

omit	only	ocean	opening	poem
hotel	clothes	clothing	dash	ranch
branch	handy	packed	package	landing
evening	fever	everyone	everybody	everything

F. Sort Your Words

1. Sometimes *ing* is an ending added to a base word. Other times *ing* is part of the base word. Write the five spelling words that end in *ing*. Of the words you have just written, circle those in which *ing* is an ending added to a base word. If you need help, use the **Spelling Dictionary**.

2. Three spelling words end with the long *e* sound. Write them. What letter makes the long *e* sound?

3. Eight spelling words have a long *o* sound. Write them in alphabetical order.

4. Seven spelling words have a short *a* sound. Write them in alphabetical order.

5. Two spelling words have not been used above. Write them.

G. Using Other Word Forms Write the Other Word Form that fits each clue.

Base Words: open(er) handy(er) poem(t) ranch(er) omit(ed)

1. more handy
2. used to open things
3. writer of poems
4. cattle farmer
5. left out

H. Challenge Words Write the Challenge Word that completes each sentence.

fractions	confessed	stroke	sweeter	talented

1. We arrived at the _____ of midnight.
2. Many actors are very _____ .
3. We learned to add whole numbers and _____ .
4. Your berries taste _____ than mine.
5. The suspect _____ to the crime.

I. Spelling and Writing Write each set of words in a sentence. You may use Other Word Forms. Proofread your work.

1. landing – ocean
2. fever – evening
3. everyone – hotel
4. omit – package
5. only – poem
6. clothing – packed
7. clothes – ranch
8. opening – dash
9. everybody – branch
10. handy – everything
11. talented – fractions
12. confessed – sweeter
13. stroke – dashed

36

■ pool	★ playmate	▲ sneakers	◆ cable	● ray
root	orange	picture	clothing	address
branch	sink	package	ocean	ranch
attic	baseball	fork	beat	tooth
pillow	stable	hotel	color	film

A. What Do You Need? Write Other Word Forms or the spelling words to complete the items. The shapes tell you in what column you can find the spelling word. Write each word or its Other Word Form only once. If you need help, use the **Spelling Dictionary**.

1. water in a swimming ■ __ __ __ __

2. friends or ★ __ __ __ __ __ __ __ __ to play tag

3. ◆ __ __ __ __ __ for trolley cars

4. the sun's ● __ __ __ __ to warm the earth

5. a ▲ __ __ __ __ __ __ __ with a shoelace that's not broken

6. fresh ★ __ __ __ __ __ __ __ to make juice

7. ◆ __ __ __ __ __ __ __ to wear to school

8. carrots with healthy ■ __ __ __ __ __

9. walls with ▲ __ __ __ __ __ __ __ __ hanging

10. numbers and streets for ● __ __ __ __ __ __ __ __ __ on letters

11. pretty paper and bows to wrap ▲ __ __ __ __ __ __ __ __

12. ovens, refrigerators, and ★ __ __ __ __ __ in kitchens

13. large farms or ● __ __ __ __ __ __ __ to raise animals

14. ■ __ __ __ __ __ __ __ __ on trees to climb

15. large ◆ __ __ __ __ __ __ for ships to sail

16. eggs that are ◆ __ __ __ __ __ __ to make breakfast

17. ● __ __ __ __ __ for chewing

18. bats and ★ __ __ __ __ __ __ __ __ __ to play a game

19. knives, ▲ __ __ __ __ __ __ , and spoons to eat a meal

20. ■ __ __ __ __ __ __ for storing old furniture

21. rooms in ▲ __ __ __ __ __ __ for travelers

22. ■ __ __ __ __ __ __ on a bed to lay your head

23. cameras for ● __ __ __ __ __ __ __ a movie

24. ◆ __ __ __ __ __ __ __ flags for the parade

25. clean ★ __ __ __ __ __ __ for horses

always	bigger	everything	July	middle
among	born	forty	June	October
another	enjoy	fourteen	leaving	only
anybody	everybody	fourth	May	since
before	everyone	gotten	means	sitting

B. Break the Code Use the code to write an Other Word Form or a spelling word. Write each word. Remember to use a capital letter for the calendar words.

a	b	c	d	e	f	g	h	i	j	k	l	m
z	y	x	w	v	u	t	s	r	q	p	o	n

1. ovzevh — leaves
2. ylim — born
3. hrgh — sits
4. qfmv — June
5. uligrvh — forties
6. nrwwov — middle
7. zmlgsvi — another
8. yvuliv — before
9. nzb — May
10. qfob — July
11. lmob — only
12. znlmthg — amongst
13. zodzbh — always

14. tvggrmt — getting
15. ulfigvvmgs — fourteenth
16. vmqlbzyov — enjoyable
17. lxglyvi — October
18. hrmxv — since
19. veviblmv — everyone
20. yrttvhg — biggest
21. nvzmrmt — meaning
22. ulfigsh — fourths
23. vevibgsrmt — everything
24. zmbylwb — anybody
25. vevibylwb — everybody

REVIEW

■ bloom	★ dream	▲ huge	◆ paste	● sank
clothes	fever	kick	poem	speak
correct	flour	mouse	pound	steam
count	fort	omit	pretend	stream
dash	hour	packed	rich	woman

C. Word Clues Write the spelling word that goes with each clue. The shapes tell you in what column you can find the spelling word. Then write an Other Word Form for each spelling word. If you need help, use the **Spelling Dictionary**.

Word Clues	Spelling Words	Other Word Forms
1. a rhyming verse ◆	— — — —	— —
2. a sticky mixture ◆	— — — — —	— —
3. to talk ●	— — — — —	— —
4. seen while sleeping ★	— — — — —	— —
5. went to the bottom ●	— — — —	— —
6. to make believe ◆	— — — — — — —	— —
7. right ■	— — — — — — —	— —
8. a blow with the foot ▲	— — — —	— —
9. a building ★	— — — —	— —
10. having a lot of money ◆	— — — —	— —
11. flowing water ●	— — — — — —	— —
12. 60 minutes ★	— — — —	— —
13. very large ▲	— — — —	— —
14. an adult female ●	— — — — —	— —
15. a small furry animal ▲	— — — — —	— —
16. to find the total ■	— — — — —	— —
17. seen from a boiling kettle ●	— — — — —	— —
18. to leave out ▲	— — — —	— —
19. a high temperature ★	— — — — —	— —
20. a fast run ■	— — — —	— —
21. filled with items ▲	— — — — — —	— —
22. worn on the body ■	— — — — — — —	— —
23. 16 ounces ◆	— — — — —	— —
24. fine powder from grain ★	— — — — —	— —
25. to flower ■	— — — — —	— —

beast	follow	loop	pouring	second
corner	handy	nearest	reader	silk
evening	happening	opening	rules	single
fallen	inches	ounce	scream	waste
feast	landing	picnic	season	windy

D. Pack Your Suitcase Add, subtract, or do both to write Other Word Forms.

+ ed

1. pouring − ing + ed = ____

2. happening − ing + ed = ____

3. landing − ing + ed = ____

4. rules − es + ed = ____

5. inches − es + ed = ____

6. opening − ing + ed = ____

+ ing

7. reader − er + ing = ____

8. fallen − en + ing = ____

9. nearest − est + ing = ____

+ est

10. silk + i + est = ____

11. windy − y + i + est = ____

12. handy − y + i + est = ____

+ s

13. feast + s = ____

14. loop + s = ____

15. beast + s = ____

16. waste + s = ____

17. follow + s = ____

18. season + s = ____

19. second + s = ____

20. corner + s = ____

21. ounce + s = ____

22. scream + s = ____

23. single + s = ____

24. picnic + s = ____

25. evening + s = ____

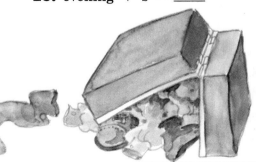

Spelling Dictionary/WORDFINDER

Your Spelling Dictionary/WORDFINDER lists all the basic spelling words and Other Word Forms in your spelling book. If the entry word is a spelling word, it is listed in **dark type**. If the entry word is not in dark type, then the spelling word is listed with the Other Word Forms at the end of the definition.

The Spelling Dictionary/WORDFINDER gives you a quick way to check the spelling and meanings of your spelling words. Because the Spelling Dictionary/WORDFINDER includes many of the words you will need in daily writing, you will find it useful for other schoolwork too.

Sample entries —

build |bĭld| *v.* To make something by putting together materials or parts: *to build a house.* **builds, built, building, buildings, builder** — Other Word Forms

built |bĭlt| *v.* Made something by putting together materials or parts: *built a bookcase.* [see *build*]

PRONUNCIATION KEY

ă	pat	j	judge	sh	dish, ship	
ā	aid, fey, pay	k	cat, kick, pique	t	tight	
â	air, care, wear	l	lid, needle	th	path, thin	
ä	father	m	am, man, mum	*th*	bathe, this	
b	bib	n	no, sudden	ŭ	cut, rough	
ch	church	ng	thing	û	circle, firm, heard,	
d	deed	ŏ	horrible, pot		term, turn, urge, word	
ĕ	pet, pleasure	ō	go, hoarse, row, toe	v	cave, valve, vine	
ē	be, bee, easy, leisure	ô	alter, caught, for, paw	w	with	
f	fast, fife, off, phase, rough	oi	boy, noise, oil	y	yes	
g	gag	ou	cow, out	yo͞o	abuse, use	
h	hat	o͝o	took	z	rose, size, xylophone, zebra	
hw	which	o͞o	boot, fruit	zh	garage, pleasure, vision	
ĭ	pit	p	pop	ə	about, silent, pencil	
ī	by, guy, pie	r	roar		lemon, circus	
î	dear, deer, fierce, mere	s	miss, sauce, see	ər	butter	

STRESS
Primary stress ´ **bi•ol´o•gy** |bī ŏl´ə jē| Secondary stress ´ **bi´o•log´i•cal** |bī´ə lŏj´ĭ kəl|

A

above |ə **bŭv´**| *prep.* Over or higher than: *above the trees.*

absent |**ăb´**sənt| *adj.* Not present: *absent students.* **absence, absently, absentee**

across |ə **krôs´**| *adv.* From one side to another: *across and over. prep.* To the other side of: *across the river.*

address |ə **drĕs´**| *n.* The place where a person lives or the place to which mail is sent: *his street address.* **addresses, addressed, addressing**

afraid |ə **frād´**| *adj.* Feeling frightened or scared: *afraid to be alone.*

again |ə **gĕn´**| *adv.* One more time: *played the game again.*

agree |ə **grē´**| *v.* To think or feel the same way as another person: *will agree that bananas are yellow.* **agrees, agreed, agreeing, agreeable, agreement**

ahead |ə **hĕd´**| *adv.* In front; farther forward: *will go ahead.*

aid |ād| *n.* Help or assistance: *thankful for their aid. v.* To help or give support to: *will aid the teacher.* **aids, aided, aiding**

alike |ə **līk´**| *adv.* In the same way: *to walk alike. adj.* The same; similar: *to be alike in many ways.* **alikeness**

almost |**ôl´**mōst| *adv.* Close to or nearly: *almost time to begin.* **most, mostly**

alone |ə **lōn´**| *adj.* Without company; by oneself: *was alone in the dark.*

already |ôl **rĕd´**ē| *adv.* By a certain time: *already finished.*

always |**ôl´** wāz| *adv.* At all times: *always sunny.*

among |ə **mŭng´**| *prep.* In the company of others: *among the animals in the zoo.* **amongst**

amount |ə **mount´**| *n.* The total or sum: *amount of snow.* **amounts, amounted, amounting**

another |ə **nŭth´**ər| *pron.* One more or a different one: *asked for another.*

anybody |**ĕn´**ē bŏd´ē| *pron.* Any person: *if anybody can go.*

apiece |ə **pēs´**| *adv.* Each; for each one: *ten cents apiece.*

arithmetic |ə **rĭth´**mətĭk| *n.* Adding, subtracting, multiplying, and dividing: *mistake in my arithmetic.* **arithmetical**

around |ə **round´**| *prep.* **1.** On the farther side of: *around the second bend.* **2.** In a circle about: *around the tree.*

attic |**ăt´**ĭk| *n.* The space just underneath the roof of a house: *stored in the attic.* **attics**

awake |ə **wāk´**| *v.* To wake up: *will awake early.* **awakes, awaked, awoke, awaking**

awoke |ə **wōk´**| *v.* Woke up: *awoke from a dream.* [see *awake*]

ax |ăks| *n.* A tool with a sharp blade, used for chopping wood: *the firefighter's ax.* **axes, axed, axing**

B

backward |**băk´**wərd| *adj.* Moving toward the rear: *backward fall.* **backwards**

banner |**băn´**ər| *n.* A flag: *a striped banner.* **banners**

baseball |**bās´**bôl´| *adj.* Of or for baseball: *baseball mitt. n.* A game played with a ball and bat by two teams with nine players on a field with four bases: *new bat for baseball.* **baseballs**

basket |bǎs′kǐt| *n.* A woven container: *a laundry basket.* **baskets**

basketball |bǎs′kǐt bôl′| *n.* A game played on a court by two teams of five players who try to toss a ball through a basket open at the bottom: *plays basketball and tennis.* **basketballs**

battle |bǎt′l| *n.* A fight: *an exciting battle.* **battles, battled, battling, battler**

be |bē| *v.* To act in a certain way: *to be late.* **am, is, are, was, were, being, been**

beast |bēst| *n.* A four-footed animal: *a wild beast.* **beasts, beastly**

beat |bēt| *n.* A stroke, blow, or sound made again and again: *beat of the band.* **beats, beaten, beating, beater**

beef |bēf| *adj.* Made of beef: *beef stew. n.* Meat from a cow, bull, or steer: *roast beef.* **beefy**

before |bǐ fôr′| *conj.* Ahead of the time when: *before you arrive.*

began |bǐ gǎn′| *v.* Started: *began to run.* [see *begin*]

begin |bǐ gǐn′| *v.* To start: *will begin to rain.* **begins, began, begun, beginning, beginner**

begun |bǐ gǔn′| *v.* Started: *since dinner has begun.* [see *begin*]

being |bē′ĭng| *v.* Acting in a certain way: *being very rude.* [see *be*]

belong |bǐ lông′| *v.* **1.** To have a proper place: *to belong here.* **2.** To be a member of: *does belong to the club.* **belongs, belonged, belonging, belongings**

belonged |bǐ lôngd′| *v.* **1.** Had a proper place: *belonged in the cupboard.* **2.** Was a member of: *belonged to our group.* [see *belong*]

bend |běnd| *v.* To curve or make crooked: *will bend the metal. n.* A part that is not straight: *a bend in the wire.* **bends, bent, bending, bendable**

between |bǐ twēn′| *prep.* In the space dividing two objects or places: *between the trees.*

bid |bǐd| *v.* To offer to pay or buy at a certain price: *will bid ten dollars.* **bids, bidding, bidder**

big |bǐg| *adj.* Large; great in amount or size: *big mountain.* **bigger, biggest**

bigger |bǐg′ər| *adj.* Larger; greater in amount or size: *a bigger piece of fruit.* [see *big*]

bind |bīnd| *v.* **1.** To fasten together between covers: *will bind these papers.* **2.** To fasten or tie together: *to bind with string or ribbon.* **binds, bound, binding, binder**

birthday |bûrth′dā′| *n.* The day on which someone is born: *fourteenth birthday.* **birthdays**

blade |blād| *n.* **1.** The metal part of an ice skate: *sharp blade on the new skate.* **2.** The flat, sharp part of an object used for cutting: *knife blade.* **blades**

blame |blām| *n.* Responsibility, or duty, for something wrong: *took the blame. v.* To find fault: *will blame you for breaking the store window.* **blames, blamed, blaming, blameful, blameless**

ă pat / ā pay / â care / ä father / ĕ pet / ē be / ĭ pit / ī pie / î fierce / ŏ pot / ō go / ô paw, for / oi oil / ŏŏ book / ōō boot / ou out / ŭ cut / û fur / *th* the / th thin / hw which / zh vision / ə ago, item, pencil, atom, circus
©1977 by Houghton Mifflin Company. Reprinted by permission from THE AMERICAN HERITAGE SCHOOL DICTIONARY.

blanket |blăng´kĭt| *n.* A woven covering used to keep people or animals warm: *a wool blanket.* **blankets, blanketed, blanketing**

blast |blăst| *n.* An explosion, or loud noise: *a blast from the mine.* **blasts, blasted, blasting**

blaze |blāz| *n.* A fire or a bright flame: *warmed by the blaze.* **blazes, blazed, blazing**

blind |blīnd| *adj.* Hidden; hard to see: *blind curve.* **blinds, blinded, blinding, blindly, blindness**

block |blŏk| *n.* Something hard and solid: *huge block of ice.* **blocks, blocked, blocking, blocker**

blocks |blŏks| *n.* More than one block: *blocks of bricks.* [see *block*]

bloom |bloom| *v.* To have or open into flowers: *will bloom in April. n.* A flower or blossom: *a spring bloom.* **blooms, bloomed, blooming, bloomer**

board |bôrd| *n.* A long, flat piece of wood used in building: *a four-foot board.* **boards, boarded, boarding, boarder**

boil |boil| *v.* To bubble and give off steam due to heating: *will boil the soup.* **boils, boiled, boiling, boiler**

born |bôrn| *adj.* Brought into life: *born on December 5.*

bother |bŏ*th*ər| *v.* To trouble, annoy, or pester: *won't bother you with any noise.* **bothers, bothered, bothering**

bound |bound| *v.* Fastened together; tied: *bound with rope.* [see *bind*]

branch |brănch| *n.* A division of a main part: *a branch of the road.* **branches, branched, branching**

brave |brāv| *adj.* Not afraid: *the brave hero.* **braver, bravest, braves, braved, braving, bravely, braveness, bravery**

break |brāk| *v.* To take or come apart: *to break a dish.* **breaks, broke, broken, breaking, breaker**

breath |brĕth| *n.* The air that goes into and comes out of the lungs: *a deep breath.—* **Out of breath**—Breathless. **breaths, breather, breathless, breathlessly, breathlessness, breathe, breathes, breathed, breathing**

brick |brĭk| *adj.* Made of bricks: *brick house. n.* A block of clay baked by sun or fire until hard: *built of brick.* **bricks, bricked, bricking**

broke |brōk| *v.* Took or came apart: *broke the dish.* [see *break*]

bruise |brooz| *n.* An injury from a fall or blow that leaves a black-and-blue mark: *arm bruise.* **bruises, bruised, bruising**

brush |brŭsh| *v.* To clean, sweep, groom, or paint with a brush: *to brush your hair.* **brushes, brushed, brushing**

bucket |bŭk´it| *n.* A round container used for carrying such things as water, sand, milk, or coal: *a bucket of sand.* **buckets**

build |bĭld| *v.* To make something by putting together materials or parts: *to build a house.* **builds, built, building, buildings, builder**

built |bĭlt| *v.* Made something by putting together materials or parts: *built a bookcase.* [see *build*]

bump |bŭmp| *n.* **1.** A small place that rises above what is around it: *a bump in the road.* **2.** A lump or swelling: *bump on his head.* **bumps, bumped, bumping, bumper, bumpy**

burn |bûrn| *v.* To set on fire: *to burn the pile of leaves*. *n.* An injury caused by fire or heat: *a burn from the hot pan*. **burns, burned, burnt, burning, burner**

busy |bĭz´e| *adj.* Active; working; having plenty to do: *busy person*. **busier, busiest, busyness**

C

cabin |kăb´ĭn| *n.* A small, plain house: *cabin made of logs*. **cabins**

cable |kā´bəl| *n.* A strong, thick rope made of twisted wire: *to pull the heavy wagon with a cable*.—**Cable car**—A car pulled by an overhead or undergound cable. **cables, cabled**

camel |kăm´əl| *n.* A large four-footed animal with either one or two humps and a long neck, found in Africa and Asia: *a camel at the zoo*. **camels**

candle |kăn´dl| *n.* A stick of wax with a wick inside: *tall, thin candle*. **candles**

can't |kănt| Contraction for *cannot*: *can't go home*.

cape |kāp| *n.* A sleeveless coat that hangs loosely from the shoulders, fastened at the neck: *a winter cape*. **capes**

care |kâr| *n.* Attention or caution: *to iron the clothes with care*. **cares, cared, caring, careless, carelessly, carelessness, careful, carefully, carefulness**

careful |kâr´fəl| *adj.* Paying attention; cautious: *a careful driver*. [see *care*]

careless |kâr´lis| *adj.* Not paying attention: *was careless and fell*. [see *care*]

case |kās| *n.* A container to hold something: *a leather case*. **cases, cased, casing**

cases |kā´sĭz| *n.* More than one case: *wooden cases for toys*. [see *case*]

cash |kăsh| *v.* To get money for: *to cash a check*. *n.* Money in the form of bills and coins: *extra cash in the bank*. **cashes, cashed, cashing, cashier**

cattle |kăt´l| *n.* Cows, bulls, and steers raised for meat and milk: *herd of cattle*.

cent |sĕnt| *n.* A penny; a coin of the United States and Canada: *one cent*. **cents**

center |sĕn´tər| *n.* The middle part or place of something: *in the center of the table*. **centers, centered, centering, central**

cents |sĕnts| *n.* More than one penny: *two cents*. [see *cent*]

chain |chān| *n.* A row of rings joined together: *a gold chain*. **chains, chained, chaining**

chance |chăns| *n.* The possibility that something will happen: *a good chance of rain*. **chances, chanced, chancing**

change |chānj| *n.* **1.** A passing from one form or place to another: *a change of weather*. **2.** Money given back when a larger amount is paid than the price of what is bought: *ten cents in change*. *v.* To put something in place of another: *will change the sheets*. **changes, changed, changing, changeable**

chart |chärt| *n.* A table, diagram, graph, etc., that gives information: *a weather chart*. **charts, charted, charting**

ă pat / ā pay / â care / ä father / ĕ pet / ē be / ĭ pit / ī pie / î fierce / ŏ pot / ō go / ô paw, for / oi oil / ŏŏ book / ŏŏ boot / ou out / ŭ cut / û fur / th the / th thin / hw which / zh vision / ə ago, item, pencil, atom, circus
©1977 by Houghton Mifflin Company. Reprinted by permission from THE AMERICAN HERITAGE SCHOOL DICTIONARY.

chase |chās| *n.* The act of following after and trying to catch: *a long chase.* *v.* To follow in order to catch: *to chase them through the woods.* **chases, chased, chasing, chaser**

check |chĕk| *n.* A written order telling a bank to pay money to the person named: *paid by check.* **checks, checked, checking, checker**

cheer |chîr| *v.* **1.** To give a shout of happiness, support, or praise: *to cheer loudly at the game.* **2.** To make or become happier: *a gift to cheer you.* **cheers, cheered, cheering, cheerful, cheerfully, cheery, cheerier, cheeriest, cheeriness**

choose |chōōz| *v.* To pick from a group: *will choose another seat.* **chooses, chose, chosen, choosing, choosy, choosier, choosiest, choosiness, chooser**

chop |chŏp| *n.* A small piece of meat with a bone: *a pork chop.* *v.* To cut by hitting with a sharp tool: *will chop the carrots for dinner.* **chops, chopped, chopping, chopper**

chose |chōz| *v.* Picked from a group: *chose a book.* [see *choose*]

clever |klĕv′ər| *adj.* Showing quick thinking; skillful: *clever idea.* **cleverer, cleverest, cleverly, cleverness**

climb |klīm| *v.* To move upward using hands and feet: *can climb a tree like a monkey.* **climbs, climbed, climbing, climber**

cloth |klôth| *n.* A piece of woven material used in making clothes: *cotton cloth.* **cloths, clothe, clothes, clothed, clothing**

clothes |klōz| *n.* Things worn to cover the body: *bought new clothes.* [see *cloth*]

clothing |klō′thĭng| *adj.* Of or for clothing: *clothing brush.* *n.* Clothes: *warm winter clothing.* [see *cloth*]

clown |kloun| *n.* A person who makes people laugh: *a circus clown.* **clowns, clowned, clowning, clownish**

club |klŭb| *adj.* Of a club: *club trip.* *n.* A group of people meeting for a special purpose: *a club at school.* **clubs, clubbed, clubbing**

coach |kōch| *n.* A teacher or trainer of athletes and performers: *our team's coach.* **coaches, coached, coaching**

coal |kōl| *n.* A black mineral used for fuel: *heats with coal.* **coals**

coin |koin| *n.* A flat, round piece of metal used as money: *a silver coin.* **coins, coined, coining, coinage**

color |kŭl′ər| *n.* One of the parts of the spectrum; a certain shade, hue, or tint: *a bright color in the painting.* **colors, colored, coloring, colorful**

copy |kŏp′ē| *v.* To make something exactly like something else: *will copy this word.* *n.* Something made to look exactly like something else: *made a copy of the letter.* **copies, copied, copying, copier**

corner |kôr′nər| *n.* The place where two surfaces or lines meet: *corner of the room.* **corners, cornered, cornering**

correct |kə rĕkt′| *adj.* Right; not having mistakes: *correct answer.* *v.* To mark the mistakes in: *will correct the test.* **corrects, corrected, correcting, correctly, correction, correctness**

count |kount| *v.* To find the total number of: *to count correctly.* **counts, counted, counting, counter**

crack |krăk| *n.* A narrow split or opening: *crack in the earth.* **cracks, cracked, cracking, cracker**

crash |krăsh| v. To fall, hit, or break suddenly with a loud noise: *will crash into the table*. n. A forceful fall, hit, or break with a loud noise: *the crash of dishes*. **crashes, crashed, crashing**

cried |krīd| v. Shed tears: *cried all night*. [see *cry*]

crime |krīm| n. An action against the law: *the crime of stealing*. **crimes, criminal**

cross |krôs| v. To draw a line across: *will cross a t*. **crosses, crossed, crossing**

crossing |krô´sĭng| v. Drawing a line across: *crossing out mistakes*. [see *cross*]

crowd |kroud| n. A large number of people gathered together: *a crowd of students*. **crowds, crowded, crowding**

cry |krī| v. To shed tears: *to cry when sad*. **cries, cried, crying, crier**

D

dance |dăns| v. To move in time to music: *likes to dance fast*. **dances, danced, dancing, dancer**

dancing |dăn´sĭng| v. Moving in time to music: *dancing the waltz*. [see *dance*]

danger |dān´jər| n. The chance of something bad happening: *was full of danger*. **dangers, dangerous, dangerously**

dare |dâr| v. To have courage to try: *to dare to escape*. n. A challenge or contest: *a dare to jump*. **dares, dared, daring, daringly**

dash |dăsh| n. A fast run: *a dash for the door*. **dashes, dashed, dashing**

dawn |dôn| n. Daybreak; the time at which daylight first appears: *left before dawn*. **dawns, dawned, dawning**

death |dĕth| n. The end of living: *the bird's death*. **deaths, deathly**

December |dĭ sĕm´bər| adj. Of December: *December storm*. n. The last and twelfth month in the year: *the first week of December*. **Dec.**

deck |dĕk| n. 1. A level on a ship: *the lower deck*. 2. A set of playing cards: *shuffled the deck*. **decks, decked, decking**

deliver |dĭ lĭv´ər| v. To carry and hand out: *to deliver the mail*. **delivers, delivered, delivering, delivery, deliverer**

demand |dĭ mănd´| v. To ask for strongly: *to demand an answer*. **demands, demanded, demanding**

didn't |dĭd´nt| Contraction for *did not*: *didn't finish*.

dim |dĭm| v. To make less bright: *to dim the headlights*. adj. Having or giving little light; not bright: *dim moonlight*. **dims, dimmed, dimming, dimmer, dimmest, dimly, dimness**

dirt |dûrt| n. Dust, mud, or any material that makes something unclean: *dirt on his face*. **dirty, dirtier, dirtiest, dirties, dirtied, dirtying**

dirty |dûr´tē| adj. Unclean: *dirty hands*. [see *dirt*]

discover |dĭ skŭv´ər| v. To find out for the first time: *might discover buried treasure*. **discovers, discovered, discovering, discoverer, discovery**

ă pat / ā pay / â care / ä father / ĕ pet / ē be / ĭ pit / ī pie / î fierce / ŏ pot / ō go / ô paw, for / oi oil / oo book / oo boot / ou out / ŭ cut / û fur / *th* the / th thin / hw which / zh vision / ə ago, item, pencil, atom, circus
©1977 by Houghton Mifflin Company. Reprinted by permission from THE AMERICAN HERITAGE SCHOOL DICTIONARY.

dive |dīv| *n.* A headfirst plunge into water: *a dive into the pool.* **dives, dived, dove, diving, diver**

draft |drăft| *n.* A flow of air: *a cold draft from the broken window.* **drafts, drafted, drafting**

drag |drăg| *v.* To pull or move slowly and heavily: *to drag the heavy box.* **drags, dragged, dragging, dragger**

drain |drān| *v.* To draw off or flow off slowly: *will drain the liquid. n.* A pipe for carrying off water or waste: *a drain for the bathroom sink.* **drains, drained, draining**

drank |drăngk| *v.* Swallowed liquids: *drank a glass of milk.* [see *drink*]

draw |drô| *v.* To pull or take out: *to draw a winning number from the hat.* **draws, drew, drawn, drawing, drawings, drawer**

dream |drēm| *n.* The pictures and thoughts seen during sleep: *had a scary dream about monsters.* **dreams, dreamed, dreamt, dreaming, dreamy, dreamer**

drill |drĭl| *n.* A tool for making holes in hard material: *the electric drill.* **drills, drilled, drilling**

drink |drĭngk| *v.* To swallow liquids: *to drink slowly.* **drinks, drank, drunk, drinking**

drive |drīv| *v.* To control the movement of a car or other vehicle: *to drive to the store for groceries.* **drives, drove, driving, driver**

driving |drī′vĭng| *v.* Controlling the movement of a car or other vehicle: *was driving a truck.* [see *drive*]

during |dŏor′ĭng| *prep.* **1.** Through the entire time of: *during the storm.* **2.** At some point of time: *during the first hour.*

E

early |ûr′lē| *adv.* At or close to the beginning of a time period: *woke early in the morning.* **earlier, earliest**

earn |ûrn| *v.* To get paid for work done: *to earn twenty dollars.* **earns, earned, earning, earnings, earner**

earth |ûrth| *n.* The planet we live on: *circled the earth.* **earthy, earthen, earthly**

eleven |ĭ lĕv′ən| *n.* A number equal to one more than ten; *eleven plus two.* **elevens, eleventh**

enjoy |ĕn joi′| *v.* To be happy with; get joy and pleasure from: *to enjoy downhill skiing.* **enjoys, enjoyed, enjoying, enjoyable, enjoyably, enjoyment**

enter |ĕn′tər| *v.* **1.** To join; become a member of: *will enter the contest.* **2.** To go or come into: *to enter the room.* **enters, entered, entering, entrance**

evening |ēv′nĭng| *n.* The time between late afternoon and early nighttime: *five o'clock in the evening.* **evenings**

event |ĭ vĕnt′| *n.* One of the contests in a program of sports: *the final event.* **events, eventful, eventfully**

everybody |ĕv′rē bŏd′ē| *pron.* All people: *everybody here.*

everyone |ĕv′rē wŭn′| *pron.* Everybody: *everyone in the room.*

everything |ĕv′rē thĭng′| *pron.* All things; *everything you bought.*

F

fade |fād| *v.* To dim; lose color: *will fade in the sun.* **fades, faded, fading**

fall |fôl| *v.* To drop from a higher place: *to fall from a ladder.* **falls, fell, falling, fallen**

fallen |fô´lən| *adj.* Down on the ground: *fallen leaves.* [see *fall*]

far |fär| *adv.* To or at a great distance: *far from home.* **farther, farthest**

farther |fär´thər| *adv.* To or at a greater distance: *farther from shore.* [see *far*]

fate |fāt| *n.* **1.** What happens to a person or thing: *the fate of snow on a warm day.* **2.** The power believed to control what will happen: *caused by fate.* **fates, fated, fateful**

fear |fîr| *v.* To feel afraid or that danger pain, or the unknown is near: *does fear the dark.* **fears, feared, fearing, fearful, fearfully, fearfulness, fearless, fearlessly, fearlessness**

fears |fîrz| *v.* Feels afraid or that danger, pain, or the unknown is near: *fears large animals.* [see *fear*]

feast |fēst| *n.* A large meal prepared for a special occasion: *cooked for the king's feast.* **feasts, feasted, feasting**

February |fĕb´roo ĕr´ē| *n.* The second month in the year: *not until February.* **Feb.**

feel |fēl| *v.* To have the sense of being: *to feel sad.* **feels, felt, feeling, feelings, feeler**

feeling |fē´lĭng| *v.* Having the sense of being: *feeling warm.* [see *feel*]

fence |fĕns| *n.* A railing or wall used to protect or mark off an area: *a wooden fence around the yard.* **fences, fenced, fencing, fencer**

fever |fē´vər| *n.* A body temperature higher than usual: *sick with a fever.* **fevers, feverish**

few |fyoo| *adj.* Not many: *a few people.* **fewer, fewest**

field |fēld| *n.* An open land with few or no trees: *ran across the field behind the school.* **fields**

film |fĭlm| *n.* A motion picture; movie: *went to see the new film.* **films, filmed, filming, filmy**

fireplace |fîr´plās´| *n.* An opening in a room for holding a fire: *burned in the fireplace.* **fireplaces**

flash |flăsh| *n.* **1.** A sudden, short blast of light: *a flash of lightning.* **2.** An instant; a split second: *happened in a flash.* **flashes, flashed, flashing, flasher, flashy**

fled |flĕd| *v.* Ran away from: *fled the fire.* [see *flee*]

flee |flē| *v.* To run away from: *to flee danger.* **flees, fled, fleeing**

flock |flŏk| *n.* A group of one kind of animal: *a flock of geese.* **flocks, flocked, flocking**

floor |flôr| *n.* **1.** The part of a room that a person stands or walks on: *a wooden floor.* **2.** A level, or story, of a building: *lives on the second floor.* **floors**

flour |flour| *n.* A fine powder made by grinding grains: *measured flour for the vanilla cake.* **flours, floured, flouring, floury**

flow |flō| *n.* Any steady, smooth movement: *the flow of the water.* **flows, flowed, flowing**

ă pat / ā pay / â care / ä father / ĕ pet / ē be / ĭ pit / ī pie / î fierce / ŏ pot / ō go / ô paw, for / oi oil / oo book /
oo boot / ou out / ŭ cut / û fur / th the / th thin / hw which / zh vision / ə ago, item, pencil, atom, circus
©1977 by Houghton Mifflin Company. Reprinted by permission from THE AMERICAN HERITAGE SCHOOL DICTIONARY.

follow |fŏl´ō| v. To go or come after: *to follow the leader.* **follows, followed, following, follower**

fond |fŏnd| adj. Loving or liking: *a fond hug.* —**Fond of**—Having a liking for. **fonder, fondest, fondly, fondness**

fork |fôrk| n. **1.** One of the parts into which something divides: *the left fork in the road.* **2.** An eating tool with a handle at one end and pointed parts at the other: *a fork and a spoon.* **forks, forked, forking**

fort |fôrt| n. A building or area that soldiers protect against an enemy: *the army's fort.* **forts, fortress, fortify**

forty |fôr´tē| adj. Four times ten: *forty pennies.* **forties, fortieth**

four |fôr| adj. One more than three: *four oranges.* **fours, fourth, fourths**

fourteen |fôr´tēn´| adj. Four more than ten: *fourteen students.* **fourteens, fourteenth**

fourth |fôrth| adj. Next after the third: *fourth grade.* [see *four*]

frame |frām| n. A form that borders something: *the window frame.* **frames, framed, framing, framer**

freeze |frēz| v. To harden into a solid by cold: *to freeze water into ice.* **freezes, froze, frozen, freezing, freezer**

fresh |frĕsh| adj. Just made or grown: *fresh bread.* **fresher, freshest, freshly, freshness**

Friday |frī´dā´| adj. Of Friday: *Friday cookout.* n. The sixth day of the week: *every Friday.* **Fri.**

fried |frīd| adj. Cooked in fat: *a pan of fried potatoes.* [see *fry*]

friend |frĕnd| n. A person someone knows and likes: *my good friend.* **friends, friendly, friendlier, friendliest**

friends |frĕndz| n. More than one friend: *his friends at school.* [see *friend*]

front |frŭnt| adj. At or near the forward part: *on the front page.* n. The part that comes first or faces forward: *the front of the room.* **fronts**

froze |frōz| v. Became hardened by cold: *when the pond froze.* [see *freeze*]

fry |frī| v. To cook in fat: *to fry eggs.* **fries, fried, frying, fryer**

G

gang |găng| n. A group of people who work or play together: *a gang of friends.* v. To form into a group: *to gang together for the trip.* —**Gang up on**—To attack as a group. **gangs, ganged, ganging**

get |gĕt| v. To be or become: *to get warmer.* **gets, got, gotten, getting**

glass |glăs| n. A hard material that breaks easily and can be seen through: *broken glass.* **glasses, glassy, glassful**

glasses |glăs´ĭz| n. A pair of glass lenses worn to help a person see better: *glasses with gold frames.* [see *glass*]

globe |glōb| n. A world map in the shape of a ball: *the globe in our classroom.* **globes, global**

glow |glō| n. A light made by a fire, star, electricity, etc.: *the glow from the bulb.* **glows, glowed, glowing**

gold |gōld| n. A bright-yellow color: *red, blue, and gold.* **golds, golden**

golden |gōl´dən| adj. Bright-yellow: *long golden hair.* [see *gold*]

gotten |gŏt´n| v. Become: *had gotten tired.* [see *get*]

gown |goun| *n.* A long dress: *a new gown for the party.* **gowns**

grandmother |grănd′mŭth′ər| *n.* The mother of one's father or mother: *visited my grandmother.* **grandmothers**

greet |grēt| *v.* To welcome in a friendly way: *to greet the guests.* **greets, greeted, greeting, greeter**

grind |grīnd| *v.* To crush into small pieces or powder: *to grind into flour.* **grinds, ground, grinding, grinder**

grip |grĭp| *n.* A tight hold or grasp: *a grip on the rope.* **grips, gripped, gripping**

grow |grō| *v.* **1.** To become: *to grow dark.* **2.** To cause to become bigger; raise: *to grow vegetables.* **grows, grew, grown, growing, growth**

grown |grōn| *v.* **1.** Become: *had grown very tall.* **2.** Caused to become bigger; raised: *had grown corn.* [see *grow*]

H

habit |hăb′ĭt| *n.* An action repeated over and over: *a habit of going to sleep early.* **habits**

hammer |hăm′ər| *n.* A tool with a metal head at the end of a long handle, used for driving nails: *a hammer and a saw.* **hammers, hammered, hammering**

handle |hăn′dl| *n.* The part of an object that is grasped or held by the hand: *the handle of the shovel.* **handles, handled, handling, handler**

handy |hăn′dē| *adj.* Easy to reach: *the handy bookshelf.* **handier, handiest, handily, handiness**

hang |hăng| *v.* To fasten to something above: *to hang your coat on the hook.* **hangs, hanged, hung, hanging, hanger**

happen |hăp′ən| *v.* To take place; occur: *to happen to us.* **happens, happened, happening**

happening |hăp′ə nĭng| *v.* Taking place; occurring: *happening tomorrow night.* [see *happen*]

harm |härm| *n.* Damage or injury: *caused harm to the forests. v.* To cause damage or injury to; hurt: *could harm you.* **harms, harmed, harming, harmful, harmless, harmlessness**

hate |hāt| *v.* To dislike very much: *to hate spiders.* **hates, hated, hating, hateful, hatefully**

hear |hîr| *v.* To take in sounds through the ear: *to hear the loud music.* **hears, heard, hearing**

heard |hûrd| *v.* Took in sounds through the ear: *heard the dog barking.* [see *hear*]

heart |härt| *n.* A red shape with rounded sides meeting in a point at the bottom and forming two curves at the top: *drew a red heart.* **hearts, hearty, heartier, heartiest**

heat |hēt| *v.* To make or become warm: *will heat our dinner.* **heats, heated, heating, heater**

heating |hē′tĭng| *v.* Making or becoming warm: *heating the milk.* [see *heat*]

heel |hēl| *n.* The piece of a shoe or boot under the back part of the foot: *a new heel for the shoe.* **heels, heeled, heeling**

ă pat / ā pay / â care / ä father / ĕ pet / ē be / ĭ pit / ī pie / î fierce / ŏ pot / ō go / ô paw, for / oi oil / o͝o book /
o͞o boot / ou out / ŭ cut / û fur / *th* the / th thin / hw which / zh vision / ə ago, item, pencil, atom, circus
©1977 by Houghton Mifflin Company. Reprinted by permission from THE AMERICAN HERITAGE SCHOOL DICTIONARY.

hero |hîr´ō| *n.* A person noted and admired for courage, bravery, etc.: *a hero in battle.* **heroes, heroic, heroism**

he's |hēz| Contraction for *he is: if he's waiting.*

high |hī| *adj.* Tall: *a high mountain.* **higher, highest, highly, highness**

higher |hī´ər| *adj.* Taller: *higher kite.* [see *high*]

highest |hī´ĭst| *adj.* Tallest: *the highest building.* [see *high*]

highway |hī´wā´| *n.* A main road: *a two-lane highway.* **highways**

hire |hīr| *v.* To pay for work: *will hire two painters.* **hires, hired, hiring**

history |hĭs´tə rē| *n.* A record of past events: *the history of Europe. adj.* Of history: *a history test.* **histories, historic, historical, historian**

hold |hōld| *v.* To take and keep in one's hands: *to hold the books.* **—Hold off—** To delay or wait. **holds, held, holding, holdings, holder**

holding |hōl´dĭng| *v.* Taking and keeping in one's hands: *holding two packages.* [see *hold*]

hole |hōl| *n.* **1.** An opening: *hole in my shirt.* **2.** A hollow place in something solid: *dug a hole.* **holes, holey**

holes |hōlz| *n.* **1.** Openings: *holes in the cloth.* **2.** Hollow places: *two holes in the wall.* [see *hole*]

homesick |hōm´sĭk´| *adj.* Sad because of being away from home: *a homesick traveler.* **homesickness**

honey |hŭn´ē| *n.* A sweet liquid made by bees: *a spoonful of honey.* **honeys, honeyed**

hope |hōp| *v.* To wish: *does hope to get a new sweater.* **hopes, hoped, hoping, hopeful, hopefully, hopefulness, hopeless, hopelessly, hopelessness**

hoping |hō´pĭng| *v.* Wishing: *hoping to win.* [see *hope*]

hotel |hō tĕl´| *n.* A building that provides rooms and food for pay: *a room at the hotel.* **hotels**

hour |our| *n.* A period of time equal to 60 minutes: *waited for an hour.* **hours, hourly, hr.**

huge |hyōōj| *adj.* Very big: *a huge canyon.* **huger, hugest, hugely, hugeness**

hundred |hŭn´drĭd| *n.* Ten times ten: *one hundred.* **hundreds, hundreth**

hung |hŭng| *v.* Fastened to something above: *hung my coat.* [see *hang*]

hunger, |hŭng´gər| *n.* The desire, or want, for food: *a hunger for vegetables.* **hungers, hungered, hungering, hungry, hungrier, hungriest, hungrily, hungriness**

hungry |hŭng´grē| *adj.* Desiring, or wanting, food: *was not very hungry.* [see *hunger*]

hunt |hŭnt| *v.* To search or look for: *to hunt buried treasure.* **hunts, hunted, hunting, hunter, hunters**

hunter |hŭn´tər| *n.* A person who hunts or searches for something: *a hunter in the hills.* [see *hunt*]

inch |ĭnch| *n.* A measure of length equal to one twelfth of a foot: *one inch of snow.* **inches, inched, inching, inching, in.**

inches |ĭnch´ĭz| *n.* More than one inch: *sixty inches tall.* [see *inch*]

indeed |ĭn dēd´| *adv.* In fact; really; truly: *is indeed pleased.*

iron |ī´ərn| *v.* To press clothes with a heated iron: *to iron the shirt. n.* A household tool with a flat bottom which is heated and used to press clothes: *unplugged the iron.* **irons, ironed, ironing**

island |ī´lənd| *n.* A piece of land surrounded by water: *sailed to the island.* **islands, islander**

it's |ĭts| Contraction for *it is: since it's cold outside.*

itself |ĭt sĕlf´| *pron.* A form used in place of *it,* often to show importance: *the monkey itself.*

J

jail |jāl| *n.* A building where people who have broken the law are kept: *the county jail.* **jails, jailed, jailing, jailer**

January |jăn´yoo ĕr´ē| *adj.* Of January: *a January vacation. n.* The first month in the year: *a birthday in January.* **Jan.**

jar |jär| *n.* A glass or clay container with a wide mouth: *a jar of jelly.* **jars, jarred, jarring**

job |jŏb| *n.* Work that has to be done: *his job to wash the dishes.* **jobs**

join |join| *v.* To meet: *to join our friends.* **joins, joined, joining, joiner**

July |joo lī´| *n.* The seventh month in the year: *going swimming in July.*

June |joon| *n.* The sixth month in the year: *the last day in June.*

K

keep |kēp| *v.* **1.** To continue in a certain place or condition: *to keep together.* **2.** To have or hold for a long time: *will keep this picture.* **keeps, kept, keeping, keeper**

kept |kĕpt| *v.* **1.** Continued in a certain place or condition: *kept quiet.* **2.** Had or held for a long time: *kept the ring in a safe place.* [see *keep*]

kick |kĭk| *n.* A blow with the foot: *a swift kick. v.* To move something by striking with the foot, or kicking: *will kick the ball.* **kicks, kicked, kicking, kicker**

knee |nē| *n.* The joint where the thigh and lower leg meet: *fell on my knee.* **knees, kneel, kneels, knelt, kneeled, kneeling**

knew |noo| *v.* **1.** Skilled in: *knew how to type.* **2.** Was sure of the facts: *knew the answer.* [see *know*]

knife |nīf| *n.* A sharp tool used for cutting: *sliced with a knife.* **knifes, knifed, knifing, knives**

knot |nŏt| *n.* A fastening made by tying together pieces of rope or string: *a knot in my shoelace.* **knots, knotted, knotting, knotty**

know |nō| *v.* **1.** To have skill in: *to know how to dance.* **2.** To be sure of the facts: *to know the exact date.* **knows, knew, known, knowing, knowingly, knowledge**

knows |nōz| *v.* **1.** Has skill in: *knows how to sing.* **2.** Is sure of the facts: *knows where you live.* [see *know*]

ă pat / ā pay / â care / ä father / ĕ pet / ē be / ĭ pit / ī pie / î fierce / ŏ pot / ō go / ô paw, for / oi oil / oo book /
oo boot / ou out / ŭ cut / û fur / th the / th thin / hw which / zh vision / ə ago, item, pencil, atom, circus
©1977 by Houghton Mifflin Company. Reprinted by permission from THE AMERICAN HERITAGE SCHOOL DICTIONARY.

L

lace |lās| *adj.* Made of lace: *lace curtains. n.* Fine threads woven in an open pattern: *trimmed with lace. v.* To fasten or tie with a string: *will lace my shoes.* **laces, laced, lacing, lacy**

ladder |lăd′ər| *n.* A piece of equipment used for climbing: *up the ladder.* **ladders**

lamb |lăm| *n.* A young sheep: *a sleeping lamb.* **lambs**

land |lănd| *n.* The surface of the earth not covered by water: *saw land from afar.* **lands, landed, landing, landings**

landing |lăn′dĭng| *n.* **1.** The platform between a set of stairs: *stopped on the landing.* **2.** A wharf or pier: *swam to the landing.* [see *land*]

late |lāt| *adv.* After the proper time: *arrived late.* **lately, later, latest, lateness**

lately |lāt′lē| *adv.* Not long ago: *have seen him lately.* [see *late*]

laugh |lăf| *v.* To make sounds that show happiness or enjoyment: *to laugh at the clown.* **laughs, laughed, laughing, laughable, laughter**

law |lô| *n.* A rule that must be followed: *obeys the law.* **laws, lawful, lawless, lawyer**

lawn |lôn| *n.* An area of grass around a house or building: *will mow the front lawn.* **—Lawn mower—**A machine for cutting grass. **lawns**

laws |lôz| *n.* More than one law: *broke no laws.* [see *law*]

lazy |lā′zē| *adj.* Not want to work or be active: *am lazy in the summer.* **lazier, laziest, lazily, laziness**

lead |lēd| *v.* To go to or be at the head of: *to lead the band.* **leads, led, leading, leader**

leading |lē′dĭng| *v.* Going to or being at the head of: *leading the race.* [see *lead*]

leaf |lēf| *n.* One of the thin, flat parts of a plant: *a leaf on the tree.* **leaves, leafy**

leak |lēk| *n.* A hole that lets something in or out by accident: *the tire with the leak.* **leaks, leaked, leaking, leaky**

lean |lēn| *v.* To rest on a person or thing for support: *to lean against the wall.* **leans, leaned, leaning, leaner, leanest**

leave |lēv| *v.* To go away: *to leave at noon.* **leaves, left, leaving**

leaving |lē′vĭng| *v.* Going away: *leaving tomorrow.* [see *leave*]

led |lĕd| *v.* Showed or guided: *led the flock of sheep.* [see *lead*]

lend |lĕnd| *v.* To let someone have or use for a time: *will lend you a sweater.* **lends, lent, lending, lender**

less |lĕs| *pron.* Fewer things or people: *has less than you do. adj.* Not a large amount of: *have less homework.* **—Much less—**Especially not. [see *little*]

lesson |lĕs′ən| *n.* Something that is learned or taught: *a spelling lesson.* **lessons**

let |lĕt| *v.* To allow: *to let him go.* **lets, letting**

letting |lĕt′ĭng| *v.* Allowing: *letting him speak.* [see *let*]

level |lĕv′əl| *adj.* At an equal height: *level with the dining table.* **levels, leveled, leveling, levelness**

lie |lī| *v.* To tell something that is not true: *to lie about where you went.* **lies, lied, lying, liar**

light |līt| *adj.* Having little weight; not heavy: *a light box.* **lights, lighted, lit, lighting, lightly, lighter, lightest, lightness**

lightly |lĭt´lē| *adv.* With little force or weight; softly: *floating lightly on air.* [see *light*]

lightning |lĭt´nĭng| *n.* A bright flash of light in the sky: *thunder and lightning.*

like |līk| *v.* To be pleased with: *to like our new neighbors.* **likes, liked, liking, likely, likelier, likeliest, likeness**

likely |līk´lē| *adj.* To be expected: *likely to be cold.* [see *like*]

little |lĭt´l| *adj.* Small; not big or large; not much: *little time to talk.* **littler, littlest, less, lesser, least, lessen, lessens, lessened, lessening**

live |lĭv| *v.* To make a home: *to live on Main Street.* **lives, lived, living**

living |lĭv´ĭng| *v.* Making a home: *living in the city.* [see *live*]

load |lōd| *n.* A thing to carry: *a load of sand.* **loads, loaded, loading, loader**

loads |lōdz| *n.* More than one load: *two loads of hay.* [see *load*]

lock |lŏk| *v.* To close with a lock: *will lock the front door.* **unlock, unlocks, unlocked, unlocking**

loop |loop| *n.* The rounded shape formed when a piece of rope or string crosses itself: *made a loop with ribbon.* **loops, looped, looping**

loud |loud| *adj.* Not quiet: *a loud bang from the cannon.* **louder, loudest, loudly, loudness**

luck |lŭk| *n.* Good fortune: *will wish you luck in the race.* **lucky, luckier, luckiest, luckily**

lucky |lŭk´ē| *adj.* Having or bringing good fortune: *a lucky penny.* [see *luck*]

lump |lŭmp| *n.* **1.** A shapeless mass: *a lump of dough.* **2.** A bump or swelling: *a lump on my hand.* **lumps, lumped, lumping, lumpy, lumpiness**

lung |lŭng| *adj.* Of the lung: *lung operation.* *n.* One of the two organs for breathing air: *left lung.* **lungs**

lying |lī´ĭng| *v.* Telling an untruth: *lying about the accident.* *adj.* Not telling the truth: *the lying thief.* [see *lie*]

M

mad |măd| *adj.* **1.** Very excited; foolish: *mad actions.* **2.** Angry: *mad for not winning.* **madder, maddest, madden, maddens, maddened, maddening, madly, madness**

madder |măd´ər| *adj.* Angrier: *madder than yesterday.* [see *mad*]

madly |măd´lē| *adv.* With great energy or power: *is working madly.* [see *mad*]

magic |măj´ĭk| *adj.* Done by using tricks to make things that seem impossible happen: *a magic wand.* **magical, magically, magician**

mail |māl| *n.* The system by which letters and packages are sent: *delivered by mail.* **mails, mailed, mailing, mailer**

mailed |māld| *v.* Sent by mail: *mailed the package.* [see *mail*]

make |māk| *v.* To put together: *to make a salad.* **makes, made, making**

ă pat / ā pay / â care / ä father / ĕ pet / ē be / ĭ pit / ī pie / î fierce / ŏ pot / ō go / ô paw, for / oi oil / o͝o book / o͞o boot / ou out / ŭ cut / û fur / *th* the / th thin / hw which / zh vision / ə ago, item, pencil, atom, circus
©1977 by Houghton Mifflin Company. Reprinted by permission from THE AMERICAN HERITAGE SCHOOL DICTIONARY.

making |mā´kĭng| v. Putting together: *making new clothes.* [see *make*]

map |măp| v. To make a map, or chart, that shows where things are located: *will map the city streets.* **maps, mapped, mapping**

mapping |măp´ĭng| v. To make a map of: *was mapping the stars in the sky.* [see *map*]

marble |mär´bəl| adj. Made of marble: *a marble tabletop.* n. A hard, polished round stone or glass: *a brightly colored marble.* **marbles, marbled, marbling**

March |märch| n. The third month in the year: *a birthday in March.* **Mar.**

mark |märk| n. A spot made on one object by another: *left a mark on the floor.* v. To show clearly: *will mark my place with this paper.* **marks, marked, marking, marker**

marker |mär´kər| n. **1.** Something used to draw or write: *paper and a blue marker.* **2.** A piece of paper, cloth, leather, etc., used to hold, or mark, one's place in a book: *found the marker on page 280.* [see *mark*]

mask |măsk| n. A covering that hides or protects the face: *a frightful mask.* **masks, masked, masking**

matter |măt´ər| v. To be important: *won't matter if we lose.* **matters, mattered**

May |mā| n. The fifth month in the year: *the first day of May.*

meal |mēl| n. Food served and eaten at one time: *a meal of meat and potatoes.* **meals**

mean |mēn| v. To intend; have as a purpose: *to mean something by her comment.* **means, meant, meaning, meaner, meanest, meaningful**

means |mēnz| v. Intends; has as a purpose: *means to do well.* [see *mean*]

meet |mēt| v. To come together by appointment: *to meet at four o'clock.* **meets, met, meeting**

meeting |mē´tĭng| n. A coming together: *a business meeting.* [see *meet*]

melt |mĕlt| v. To turn into a liquid by heating: *to melt wax.* **melts, melted, melting**

middle |mĭd´l| n. The point equally distant between two sides or times; center: *middle of the room.*

might |mīt| n. Great power, strength, or skill: *the might of the storm.* **mighty, mightier, mightiest**

mighty |mī´tē| adj. Powerful, strong, or skillful: *a mighty lion.* [see *might*]

mild |mīld| adj. Not very hot or cold: *a mild winter.* **milder, mildest, mildly, mildness**

mile |mīl| n. A measure of distance equal to 5,280 feet: *drove for one mile.* **miles, mileage**

mint |mĭnt| n. A plant used for flavoring: *lemonade with mint.* **mints, minted, minting, minty**

mist |mĭst| n. Very fine drops of water in the air: *mist on the windshield.* **mists, misted, misting, misty**

mix |mĭks| v. To combine together by stirring: *to mix flour, water, and eggs.* **mixes, mixed, mixing, mixer, mixture**

Monday |mŭn´dā| n. The second day of the week: *starts school on Monday.* **Mon.**

monster |mŏn´stər| n. An imaginary creature that is very large and frightening: *saw an ugly monster.* **monsters, monstrous, monstrosity**

month |mŭnth| n. One of twelve periods of time in a year: *the month of January.* **months, monthly**

mostly |mōst′lē| *adv.* Mainly; for the most part: *mostly cloudy.* [see *much*]

mouse |mous| *n.* A small furry animal with a long tail: *a gray mouse.* **mice, mousy**

much |mŭch| *adv.* Greatly: *not much pleased with the painting.* **more, most, mostly**

music |myoo′zĭk| *n.* An interesting or pleasing combination of sounds: *loud music.* **musical, musically, musician**

N

nail |nāl| *n.* A thin, pointed piece of metal used to hold things together: *will hammer the nail.* **nails, nailed, nailing**

nails |nālz| *n.* More than one nail: *tools and nails.* [see *nail*]

near |nîr| *adj.* Close by in space or time: *in the near future.* **nears, neared, nearing, nearer, nearest, nearness, nearly**

nearest |nîr′ĭst| *adj.* Closest: *the nearest exit.* [see *near*]

nineteen |nĭn′tēn′| *adj.* Nine more than ten: *nineteen people. n.* Nine more than ten: *a group of nineteen.* **nineteens, nineteenth**

nobody |nō′bŏd′ē| *pron.* No person: *nobody allowed inside.*

noise |noiz| *n.* A loud and unpleasant sound: *too much noise.* **noises, noisy, noisier, noisiest, noisily, noisiness**

none |nŭn| *pron.* Not any: *have none left.*

notebook |nōt′books′| *n.* A book with blank pages on which to write: *wrote a poem in my notebook.* **notebooks**

notebooks |nōt′books′| *n.* More than one notebook: *bought two notebooks for school.* [see *notebook*]

November |nō vĕm′bər| *n.* The eleventh month in the year: *took a vacation in November.* **Nov.**

number |nŭm′bər| *n.* **1.** A numeral connected with a person or thing: *telephone number.* **2.** A numeral: *the next number.* **numbers, numbered, numbering**

nurse |nûrs| *n.* A person trained to take care of people who are sick: *the doctor and the nurse.* **nurses, nursed, nursing, nursery**

O

oak |ōk| *adj.* Made of wood from an oak tree: *an oak floor. n.* **1.** A tree with strong wood and acorns: *the oak in the yard.* **2.** The wood from an oak tree: *a chair of oak.* **oaks**

ocean |ō′shən| *n.* One of the large bodies of salt water that covers almost all of the earth's surface: *swam in the ocean.* **oceans**

o'clock |ə klŏk′| *adv.* According to the clock: *begins at two o'clock.*

October |ŏk tō′bər| *adj.* Of October: *an October holiday. n.* The tenth month in the year: *a day in October.* **Oct.**

oil |oil| *n.* A greasy substance that does not mix with water: *a can of oil.* **oils, oiled, oiling, oily**

old |ōld| *adj.* Not young: *an old tree.* **older, oldest**

ă pat / ā pay / â care / ä father / ĕ pet / ē be / ĭ pit / ī pie / î fierce / ŏ pot / ō go / ô paw, for / oi oil / oo book / oo boot / ou out / ŭ cut / û fur / *th* the / th thin / hw which / zh vision / ə ago, item, pencil, atom, circus
©1977 by Houghton Mifflin Company. Reprinted by permission from THE AMERICAN HERITAGE SCHOOL DICTIONARY.

oldest |ōl′dĭst| *adj.* Having lived for the longest time: *oldest brother.* [see *old*]

omit |ō mĭt′| *v.* To leave out: *to omit the salt.* **omits, omitted, omitting**

only |ōn′lē| *adj.* By itself; one and no more: *the only window.*

open |ō′pən| *v.* To make or become not shut: *to open the door.* **opens, opened, opening, openings, openly, opener**

opening |ō′pə nĭng| *n.* A hole: *covered the opening.* [see *open*]

orange |ôr′ĭnj| *n.* A reddish-yellow citrus fruit: *ate an orange.* **oranges**

ounce |ouns| *n.* A measure of weight equal to one sixteenth of a pound: *one ounce of cheese.* **ounces, oz.**

outfit |out′fĭt′| *n.* All the articles or clothing necessary for a special purpose: *a skiing outfit.* **outfits, outfitted, outfitting, outfitter**

outfits |out′fĭts′| *n.* More than one outfit: *outfits for hiking.* [see *outfit*]

own |ōn| *v.* To have: *does own a bicycle.* **owns, owned, owning, owner, owners**

owner |ō′nər| *n.* A person who owns: *owner of the lost cat.* [see *own*]

P

pack |păk| *v.* To fill with items: *to pack a suitcase.* **packs, packed, packing, packer**

package |păk′ĭj| *n.* A group of items packed or wrapped together: *mailed a package.* **packages, packaged, packaging**

packed |păkt| *v.* Filled with items: *packed the box.* [see *pack*]

paddle |păd′l| *v.* To move a boat with a short oar: *to paddle across the lake. n.* A piece of wood with a handle at one end, used for mixing, stirring, etc.: *a paddle for stirring cement.* **paddles, paddled, paddling, paddler**

pain |pān| *n.* A feeling of hurt caused by an injury or sickness: *felt a sudden and sharp pain.* **pains, painful, painfully, painfulness, painless, painlessly, painlessness**

part |pärt| *n.* Not all: *part of the problem.* **parts, parted, parting, partner, partly**

partly |pärt′lē| *adv.* In part; in some measure or degree: *partly to blame.* [see *part*]

party |pär′tē| *n.* A group of people gathered together to have fun: *played games at the party.* **parties, partied, partying**

paste |pāst| *n.* A thick mixture used to stick things together: *has used paste to put photos in the album.* **pastes, pasted, pasting, pasty**

peek |pēk| *v.* To look at secretly: *to peek into the room.* **peeks, peeked, peeking**

phone |fōn| *n.* An instrument for sending and receiving speech over long distances; a telephone: *talked on the phone.* **phones, phoned, phoning**

picnic |pĭk′nĭk| *adj.* Of or for a picnic: *picnic lunch. n.* A meal that is eaten outside: *made salad for the picnic.* **picnics, picnicked, picnicking, picnicker**

picture |pĭk′chər| *n.* A drawing, painting, or photograph of someone or something: *a picture of my family.* **pictures, pictured, picturing**

pile |pīl| *n.* A large amount of things stacked on top of each other: *a pile of clothes.* **piles, piled, piling**

pillow |pĭl´ō| n. A stuffed cloth case that is used to support a person's head while lying down: *a pillow on the bed.* **pillows**

plane |plān| n. A machine with propellers or jet engines that make it fly; an airplane: *landed the plane.* **planes**

playmate |plā´māt´| n. A person who plays with someone else: *playmate in the neighborhood.* **playmates**

plenty |plĕn´tē| n. A full supply of all that is needed: *plenty of water.* **plentiful, plentifully**

plum |plŭm| n. A juicy purple fruit with a smooth skin and a pit: *a plum and a pear.* **plums**

pocket |pŏk´ĭt| n. A small bag for holding things, sewn into clothing: *keys in her pocket.* **pockets, pocketed, pocketing, pocketful**

poem |pō´əm| n. A form of writing with words arranged in verses that often rhyme: *a poem about summer.* **poems, poet, poetry**

point |point| n. The main purpose or idea: *understood the point you made.* **points, pointed, pointing, pointless, pointer**

pool |pōōl| n. A tank of water for swimming: *swam to the edge of the pool.* **pools**

porch |pôrch| n. A covered area built onto a house: *on the front porch.* **porches**

post |pōst| n. A straight piece of wood or metal used to hold something up: *nailed to the post.* **posts, posted, posting**

poster |pō´stər| n. A large printed notice put out for the public to see: *a circus poster.* **posters**

pound |pound| n. A unit of weight equal to sixteen ounces: *one pound of fish.* **pounds, pounded, pounding, lb.**

pour |pôr| v. To flow or cause to flow steadily: *to pour milk.* **pours, poured, pouring**

pouring |pôr´ĭng| v. Flowing or causing to flow steadily: *pouring from the hose.* adj. Flowing: *pouring rain.* [see *pour*]

power |pou´ər| adj. Run by a motor: *a power drill.* n. Strength: *the power of five people.* **powers, powered, powering, powerful, powerfully**

press |prĕs| n. A machine for printing books, magazines, and newspapers: *operated the press.* v. To put force on something: *to press the door shut.* **presses, pressed, pressing**

pretend |prĭ tĕnd´| v. To make believe: *to pretend you are flying.* **pretends, pretended, pretending, pretender**

price |prīs| n. The cost or amount of money for which something is bought or sold: *for the same price.* **prices, priced, pricing**

prices |prī´sĭz| n. Costs; *low prices for gas.* [see *price*]

pride |prīd| n. Pleasure in one's actions or worth; self-respect: *takes pride in her schoolwork.* **prides, prided, priding, prideful**

print |prĭnt| n. Letters in ink, stamped by type: *easy-to-read print.* v. To write in block letters, like those seen in print: *will print my name.* **prints, printed, printing, printer**

prize |prīz| n. An award won in a contest or game: *tried to win the prize.* **prizes, prized, prizing**

ă pat / ā pay / â care / ä father / ĕ pet / ē be / ĭ pit / ī pie / î fierce / ŏ pot / ō go / ô paw, for / oi oil / ŏŏ book / ōō boot / ou out / ŭ cut / û fur / th the / th thin / hw which / zh vision / ə ago, item, pencil, atom, circus
©1977 by Houghton Mifflin Company. Reprinted by permission from THE AMERICAN HERITAGE SCHOOL DICTIONARY.

proud |proud| *adj.* Feeling very pleased or satisfied: *a proud winner.* **prouder, proudest, proudly**

provide |prə vīd′| *v.* **1.** To prepare ahead of time: *to provide lunch and dinner.* **2.** To give what is needed: *will provide pens and paper.* **provides, provided, providing, provider**

purse |pûrs| *n.* A handbag or pocketbook: *a leather purse.* **purses**

Q

queen |kwēn| *n.* A female monarch, or ruler; a king's wife: *the queen on her throne.* **queens, queenly**

quiet |kwī′ĭt| *adj.* Peaceful; with little noise: *a quiet time.* **quieter, quietest, quietly, quiteness**

quit |kwĭt| *v.* **1.** To give up: *to quit the team.* **2.** To stop: *will quit painting my room before noon.* **quits, quitted, quitting, quitter**

quite |kwīt| *adv.* Completely: *quite clear.*

R

race |rās| *n.* A contest to find the fastest: *an automobile race.* **races, raced, racing, racer**

races |rā′sĭz| *n.* More than one race: *bicycle races.* [see *race*]

rack |răk| *n.* A bar or stand on which to hang things: *a metal rack for clothes.* **racks**

rain |rān| *v.* To fall in drops of water from clouds: *to rain heavily.* **rains, rained, raining, rainy, rainier, rainiest**

rainy |rā′nē| *adj.* Having rain: *a rainy afternoon.*—**Rainy day**—A time of need in the future. [see *rain*]

ranch |rănch| *n.* A large farm for raising animals: *herds of cattle at the ranch.*—**Ranch house**—A one-story house. **ranches, rancher**

range |rānj| *v.* To travel, wander, or roam over a wide area: *will range from place to place.* **ranges, ranged, ranging, ranger, rangers**

ranger |rān′jər| *n.* A person who guards a forest or park: *the park ranger.* [see *range*]

ray |rā| *n.* A narrow beam of light: *a bright ray.* **rays**

read |rēd| *v.* To look at something written and understand the meaning: *to read the headlines and the editorials in the newspaper.* **reads, reading, reader, readers**

reader |rē′dər| *n.* A person who reads: *a reader of poetry, plays, and short stories.* [see *read*]

real |rē′əl| *adj.* **1.** True; not made up: *the real story.* **2.** Not imitation or fake: *real flowers.* **really, realize, realist, realistic**

recover |rĭ kŭv′ər| *v.* To get back something lost or stolen: *to recover the missing wallet.* **recovers, recovered, recovering, recovery**

remind |rĭ mīnd′| *v.* To make a person remember something: *to remind him of the meeting.* **reminds, reminded, reminding, reminder**

repair |rĭ pâr′| *v.* To mend or fix: *to repair the damage.* **repairs, repaired, repairing, repairer**

replace |rĭ plās′| *v.* To fill or take the place of: *will replace the exact number of eggs I use.* **replaces, replaced, replacing, replacement**

return |rĭ **tûrn´**| *v.* To bring, send, put, or give back: *to return the lost wallet.* **returns, returned, returning, returnable**

returning |rĭ **tûr´**nĭng| *v.* Bringing, sending, putting, or giving back: *was returning what I borrowed.* [see *return*]

reward |rĭ **wôrd´**| *n.* **1.** Money given or offered for the return of something lost, the capture of a criminal, information, etc.: *received a ten-dollar reward for finding the lost kitten.* **2.** Something given or received in return for doing something; a prize: *got a reward for rescuing the child.* **rewards, rewarded, rewarding**

rich |rĭch| *adj.* Having a lot of money or wealth: *a rich uncle.* **richer, richest, richly, riches**

ripe |rīp| *adj.* Completely grown and ready for eating: *ripe fruit.* **riper, ripest, ripen, ripens, ripened, ripening, ripeness**

river |rĭv´ər| *n.* A natural stream of water that flows into another body of water: *floating down to the river.* **rivers**

roar |rôr| *n.* A loud, deep sound: *the animal's roar.* **roars, roared, roaring, roarer**

roll |rōl| *v.* To turn over and over: *to roll the ball across the floor.* **rolls, rolled, rolling, roller**

rolled |rōld| *v.* Turned over and over: *rolled down the stairs.* [see *roll*]

root |rōot| *n.* The part of a plant that grows underground: *dug down the root.* **roots, rooted, rooting**

rule |rool| *n.* A statement of what should and should not be done: *one rule of the game.* **rules, ruled, ruling, ruler**

rules |roolz| *n.* More than one rule: *followed the rules.* [see *rule*]

S

sack |săk| *n.* A large bag made of rough cloth: *stuffed dirty clothes into a sack.* **sacks**

saddle |săd´l| *n.* A seat for riding on the back of a horse or similar animal: *a leather saddle.* **saddles, saddled, saddling, saddler**

sail |sāl| *n.* A piece of material that catches the wind to make a boat move: *raised the sail much higher.* **sails, sailed, sailing, sailor**

sank |săngk| *v.* Went under the surface of or to the bottom of some liquid: *sank in the pond.* [see *sink*]

Saturday |săt´ər dā´| *n.* The seventh day of the week: *soccer practice on Saturday.* **Sat.**

save |sāv| *v.* **1.** To set aside or store up for future use: *to save money.* **2.** To rescue or protect from danger: *to save him from the fire.* **saves, saved, saving, savings, saver**

saves |sāvz| *v.* **1.** Sets aside or stores up for future use: *saves all kinds of buttons.* **2.** Rescues or protects from danger: *saves people from burning buildings.* [see *save*]

scale |skāl| *n.* **1.** A series of musical tones: *played a scale on the piano.* **2.** One of the thin, hard parts that covers the outside of fish and reptiles: *a scale from the fish.* **scales, scaled, scaling, scaly**

scold |skōld| *v.* To blame angrily: *to scold for arriving late.* **scolds, scolded, scolding**

ă pat / ā pay / â care / ä father / ĕ pet / ē be / ĭ pit / ī pie / î fierce / ŏ pot / ō go / ô paw, for / oi oil / o͝o book / o͞o boot / ou out / ŭ cut / û fur / *th* the / th thin / hw which / zh vision / ə ago, item, pencil, atom, circus
©1977 by Houghton Mifflin Company. Reprinted by permission from THE AMERICAN HERITAGE SCHOOL DICTIONARY.

score |skôr| *n.* The total points made in a game, test, or contest: *a score of 90.* **scores, scored, scoring, scorer**

scrap |skrăp| *n.* A small piece: *a scrap of paper.* **scraps**

scrape |skrāp| *v.* To smooth or clean by rubbing: *to scrape your boots. n.* A scratched or scraped place: *a scrape on my knee.* **scrapes, scraped, scraping, scraper**

scream |skrēm| *n.* A loud, sharp cry or sound: *heard a scream.* **screams, screamed, screaming, screamer**

scrub |skrŭb| *v.* To wash by rubbing: *to scrub your face.* **scrubs, scrubbed, scrubbing, scrubber**

season |sē′zən| *n.* One of the four parts in a year; spring, summer, fall, or winter: *a snowy season.* **seasons, seasoned, seasoning, seasonal**

seat |sēt| *n.* A place to sit: *an empty seat.* **seats, seated, seating**

second |sĕk′ənd| *n.* One of sixty periods of time in a minute: *lasts only one second. adj.* After the first: *second door on the left.* **seconds, seconded, seconding, secondly**

seem |sēm| *v.* To appear to be be: *to seem happy.* **seems, seemed, seeming**

seemed |sēmd| *v.* Appeared to be: *seemed pleased.* [see *seem*]

sense |sĕns| *n.* Good judgment; intelligence: *didn't use very much sense.* **senses, sensed, sensing, senseless**

September |sĕp tĕm′bər| *n.* The ninth month in the year: *the beginning of September.* **Sept.**

seven |sĕv′ən| *adj.* One more than six: *seven cats.* **sevens, seventh, sevenths**

seventh |sĕv′ənth| *adj.* Next after the sixth: *the seventh grade.* [see *seven*]

shake |shāk| *v.* **1.** To move quickly from side to side or up and down: *to shake in the wind.* **2.** To grasp hands in greeting another person: *to shake firmly.* **shakes, shook, shaking, shaky, shakier, shakiest, shakily, shaker**

shame |shām| *n.* A. fact to be sorry about: *a shame to miss the party.* **shames, shamed, shaming, shameless, shamelessness, shameful**

shape |shāp| *n.* A form: *the shape of a ball.* **shapes, shaped, shaping, shapeless, shapely**

share |shâr| *n.* **1.** A part given or belonging to one person: *an equal share. v.* To divide and give away in parts: *to share an orange.* **2.** To use with others: *will share the same room.* **shares, shared, sharing, sharer**

sharing |shâr′ĭng| *v.* Using with others: *sharing our books.* [see *share*]

shed |shĕd| *n.* A small building used for storage: *tools in the shed.* **sheds, shedding**

sheep |shēp| *n.* An animal with thick wool and hooves: *sheep in the meadow.* **sheepish**

sheet |shēt| *n.* A large piece of cloth used to cover a bed: *slept under the sheet.* **sheets**

shell |shĕl| *n.* The hard outer covering of some animals: *The turtle's shell.* **shells, shelled, shelling**

she's |shēz| Contraction for *she is: since she's late.*

shine |shīn| *n.* Brightness: *the shine from the flashlight. v.* To make bright; polish: *to shine with a clean cloth.* **shines, shined, shone, shining, shiny, shinier, shiniest**

shining |shī´nĭng| v. Making bright; polishing: *is shining shoes.* adj. Bright: *shining star.* [see *shine*]

shirt |shûrt| n. A piece of clothing worn on the upper part of the body: *buttoned my shirt.* **shirts**

shock |shŏk| n. **1.** A sudden feeling caused by electricity passing through the body: *a shock from the loose wire.* **2.** A sudden, upsetting happening: *was a shock to me.* **shocks, shocked, shocking, shockingly**

shore |shôr| n. The land along the edge of an ocean, river, or lake: *shells on the shore.* **shores**

shout |shout| n. A loud call or cry: *a shout of joy when the parade began.* **shouts, shouted, shouting**

show |shō| v. To put in sight; let be seen: *to show her stamp collection.* **shows, showed, shown, showing**

shower |shou´ər| n. **1.** A bath in which water sprays down on a person: *used soap in the shower.* **2.** A brief fall of rain: *an afternoon shower.* **showers, showered, showering**

shown |shōn| v. Put in sight; let be seen: *had shown me his new navy-blue coat.* [see *show*]

sidewalk |sīd´wôk´| n. A place by the edge of a street where people can walk: *stepped over every big crack in the sidewalk.* **sidewalks**

sideways |sīd´wāz| adv. With one side facing forward: *stepped sideways through the crowd.*

silk |sĭlk| n. A soft, shiny material: *a jacket lined with silk.* adj. Made of silk: *a silk tie.* **silks, silky, silkier, silkiest, silken**

silver |sĭl´vər| n. A soft, shiny white metal: *made of silver.* adj. Shiny gray: *a silver crayon.* **silvers, silvered, silvery**

since |sĭns| prep. From a past time until now: *since last month.*

single |sĭng´gəl| adj. Only one: *a single sheet of paper.* —**Single file**—A line of people or things arranged one behind the other. **singles, singly, singular**

sink |sĭngk| v. To go under the surface of or to the bottom of some liquid: *will sink in the ocean.* n. A shallow tub used for washing: *a sink filled with water.* **sinks, sank, sunk, sunken, sinking**

sir |sûr| n. A title used instead of a man's name: *sir or madam.* **sirs**

sit |sĭt| v. To rest with the back upright and the weight off the feet: *to sit in a chair.* **sits, sat, sitting, sitter**

sitting |sĭt´ĭng| v. Resting upright: *sitting on a bench.* [see *sit*]

six |sĭks| adj. One more than five: *six apples.* **sixes, sixth, sixths**

sixteen |sĭks´tēn´| adj. Six more than ten: *sixteen years old.* n. Six more than ten: *a group of sixteen.* **sixteens, sixteenth**

sixth |sĭksth| adj. Next after the fifth: *the sixth person.* n. The next after the fifth: *the sixth in line.* [see *six*]

size |sīz| n. **1.** The height, length, and width of something: *the size of our house.* **2.** A series of measurements used for things made, such as clothes: *took a smaller size.* **sizes, sized, sizing**

ă pat / ā pay / â care / ä father / ĕ pet / ē be / ĭ pit / ī pie / î fierce / ŏ pot / ō go / ô paw, for / oi oil / oŏ book /
oō boot / ou out / ŭ cut / û fur / *th* the / th thin / hw which / zh vision / ə ago, item, pencil, atom, circus
©1977 by Houghton Mifflin Company. Reprinted by permission from THE AMERICAN HERITAGE SCHOOL DICTIONARY.

skate |skāt| *n.* A special shoe that has metal blade or small wheels for gliding over smooth surfaces: *laced my skate.* *v.* To move on skates: *to skate in a circle.* **skates, skated, skating, skater**

skating |skā´tĭng| *adj.* Of skating: *skating skirt.* *v.* Moving on skates: *was skating with friends.* [see *skate*]

skill |skĭl| *n.* The ability to do something well through training and practice: *has skill in spelling.* **skills, skilled, skillful, skillfully, skillfullness**

sleep |slēp| *v.* To rest the body and mind: *to sleep at night.* **sleeps, slept, sleeping, sleepy, sleepier, sleepiest, sleepily, sleeper**

sleepy |slē´pē| *adj.* Needing or ready for sleep: *sleepy child.* [see *sleep*]

slept |slĕpt| *v.* Rested the body and mind: *slept for eight hours.* [see *sleep*]

slice |slīs| *v.* To cut into thin, flat pieces: *to slice meat.* **slices, sliced, slicing, slicer**

sliced |slīst| *adj.* In thin, flat pieces: *ate sliced cheese.* *v.* Cut into thin, flat pieces: *sliced a loaf of bread.* [see *slice*]

slid |slĭd| *v.* Moved easily: *slid into third base.* [see *slide*]

slide |slīd| *n.* A smooth surface for moving easily on: *a metal slide in the playground.* *v.* To move easily: *to slide down the hill.* **slides, slid, sliding, slider**

sliding |slī´dĭng| *adj.* Moving easily: *sliding window.* *v.* Moving easily: *was sliding on skis.* [see *slide*]

slip |slĭp| *v.* To slide suddenly without control: *to slip on the ice.* **slips, slipped, slipping, slippery, slipper, slippers, slipperiness**

slow |slō| *adj.* Not moving quickly: *a slow train on the track.* **slows, slower, slowest, slowed, slowing, slowly, slowness**

slowly |slō´lē| *adv.* Not quickly: *drove slowly.* [see *slow*]

smile |smīl| *v.* To show happiness or amusement: *to smile with delight.* *n.* An expression on the face showing that a person is happy or amused: *a big smile from every student.* **smiles, smiled, smiling, smiler**

smoke |smōk| *n.* A cloud of gas given off by something burning: *smoke from the fire.* **smokes, smoked, smoking, smoker, smoky, smokier, smokiest**

snap |snăp| *v.* To break with a sudden, sharp sound: *will snap the small twig in half.* **snaps, snapped, snapping, snapper**

sneaker |snē´kər| *n.* A canvas shoe with a rubber sole: *found the matching sneaker.* **sneakers**

sneakers |snē´kərz| *n.* More than one sneaker: *white sneakers for tennis.* [see *sneaker*]

sob |sŏb| *n.* The act or sound of crying with gasps of breath: *heard the child's sob.* *v.* To cry with gasps of breath: *will sob when sad.* **sobs, sobbed, sobbing**

soil |soil| *n.* Dirt: *growing in soil.* **soils, soiled, soiling**

sore |sôr| *adj.* Painful; tender: *soothed my sore toe.* **sores, sorely, sorer, sorest, soreness**

sort |sôrt| *n.* A kind; type: *this sort of animal.* **sorts, sorted, sorting, sorter**

space |spās| *n.* **1.** The region beyond the earth's atmosphere: *a rocket in space.* **2.** A limited place or area: *little space in the tent.* **spaces, spaced, spacing, spacer**

speak |spēk| *v.* To say words: *to speak very softly.* **speaks, spoke, spoken, speaking, speaker**

spend |spĕnd| *v.* **1.** To pay out: *will spend five dollars.* **2.** To use up: *to spend more energy.* **spends, spent, spending, spender**

spin |spĭn| *v.* To turn around quickly: *to spin until dizzy. n.* A quick turn: *one more spin.* **spins, spun, spinning, spinner**

spoke |spōk| *v.* Said words: *spoke to the teacher.* [see *speak*]

sport |spôrt| *n.* A game in which a person exercises: *the sport of basketball.* **sports, sporting**

stable |stā′bəl| *n.* A building where horses and cattle are kept: *hay in the stable.* **stables, stabled**

stake |stāk| *n.* A stick driven into the ground for holding or marking something: *a stake for the badminton net.* **stakes, staked, staking**

steal |stēl| *v.* To take something that belongs to someone else: *since robbers steal valuables.* **steals, stole, stolen, stealing**

steam |stēm| *n.* Hot water in the form of gas or mist: *steam from the boiling kettle.* **steams, steamed, steaming, steamy, steamer**

steel |stēl| *adj.* Made of steel: *a steel bridge. n.* A hard and strong metal: *tools made from steel.* **steels, steely**

steep |stēp| *adj.* Having an almost straight up-and-down slope: *climbed a steep hill.* **steeper, steepest**

stocking |stŏk′ĭng| *n.* A knitted covering for the leg and foot: *wore a silk stocking.* **—In one's stocking feet—**Wearing stockings without shoes. **stocking**

stole |stōl| *v.* Took something dishonestly: *stole money.* [see *steal*]

stories |stôr′ēz| *n.* More than one story: *stories about history.* [see *story*]

story |stôr′ē| *n.* A tale about something that has happened, either true or made up: *a funny story.* **stories**

strange |strānj| *adj.* Unusual; odd: *a strange noise.* **stranger, strangest, strangely, strangeness**

straw |strô| *n.* Dry stalks of grain: *straw for the horses.* **straws**

stream |strēm| *n.* A small body of flowing water: *fished in the stream for large trout.* **streams, streamed, streaming, streamer**

strike |strīk| *v.* **1.** To stop work for better pay, shorter hours, etc.: *workers who will strike next week.* **2.** To hit: *will strike it with your fist.* **—Strike out—**In baseball, to pitch three strikes to a batter, putting the batter out. **strikes, struck, striking, striker**

strong |strông| *adj.* Having a great amount of strength or power: *a strong bear.* **stronger, strongest, strongly**

study |stŭd´ē| v. To try to learn: *to study science.* **studies, studied, studying, studious, student**

sum |sŭm| n. **1.** An amount of money: *a sum of five dollars.* **2.** The number gotten from adding two or more numbers together: *to find the sum of 2 plus 6 plus 13.* **sums, summed, summing, summary**

Sunday |sŭn´dā| adj. Of Sunday: *Sunday dinner.* n. The first day of the week: *a picnic on Sunday.* **Sun.**

sure |shoor| adj. Certain: *is sure it will rain.* **surer, surest, surely**

sweep |swēp| v. To clear or take away: *to sweep the dust.* **sweeps, swept, sweeping, sweeper**

swift |swĭft| adj. Moving very fast: *a swift swimmer in the race.* **swifter, swiftest, swiftly**

swim |swĭm| v. To move in water by using arms, legs, or fins: *will swim in the lake.* **swims, swam, swum, swimming, swimmer**

swing |swĭng| n. A seat hung from ropes in which a person can sit and move back and forth: *the swing at the park.* **swings, swung, swinging, swinger**

sword |sôrd| n. A weapon with a long sharp blade attached to a handle: *the knight's sword.* **swords**

T

team |tēm| n. A group of people playing or working together: *a hockey team.* **teams, teamed, teaming**

tear |tîr| n. A drop of liquid coming from the eye: *wiped away a tear.* **tears, teared, tearing, tearful**

tear |târ| v. To make a hole by ripping: *to tear a sleeve.* **tears, tore, torn, tearing**

teeth |tēth| n. More than one tooth: *white teeth.* [see *tooth*]

tend |tĕnd| v. To be likely: *to tend to sleep late.* **tends, tended, tending, tender**

thick |thĭk| adj. Having much space between two sides: *thick doors and walls.* — **Through thick and thin**—In both good and bad times. **thicker, thickest, thickly, thickness**

thousand |thou´zənd| adj. Ten times one hundred: *earned a thousand dollars.* **thousands, thousandth**

thread |thrĕd| n. Thin strands, or lengths, of spun and twisted cotton, silk, nylon, etc., used for sewing: *blue thread for sewing the shirt.* **threads, threaded, threading, threader**

throw |thrō| n. A toss: *a throw to the catcher.* v. To send through the air; toss: *will throw the ball.* **throws, threw, thrown, throwing, thrower**

ticket |tĭk´ĭt| n. **1.** A card or paper that gives certain rights to the person who holds it: *a ticket to the circus.* **2.** A tag or label attached to something to show a price, tell who owns it, etc.: *a ticket sewn on a shirt.* **tickets, ticketed, ticketing**

tin |tĭn| n. A soft silver-white metal: *a box made of tin.* **tins, tinned, tinning, tinny**

tiny |tī´nē| adj. Very small: *a tiny kitten.* **tinier, tiniest**

tire |tīr| v. To make or become weary: *to tire after running.* **tires, tired, tiring, tireless, tiresome**

tired |tīrd| *adj.* Weary, or worn out: *too tired to stay awake.* [see *tire*]

ton |tŭn| *n.* A unit of weight equal to 2,000 pounds: *weighed a ton.* **tons**

tooth |tōoth| *n.* One of the hard, bony parts in the mouth, used for chewing and biting: *one loose tooth.* **teeth, toothy**

tore |tôr| *v.* Made a hole by ripping: *tore the cloth.* [see *tear*]

tower |tou′ər| *n.* A tall building: *the bell in the tower.* **towers, towered, towering**

trace |trās| *n.* **1.** A small amount: *a trace of dirt.* **2.** A drawing done by tracing: *a trace of the circle. v.* To copy by drawing over lines seen through thin paper: *to trace a picture.* **traces, traced, tracing, tracer**

trap |trăp| *n.* A trick used to catch a person by surprise: *a sneaky trap.* **traps, trapped, trapping, trapper**

tribe |trīb| *n.* A group of people with the same ancestors and traditions: *from the same tribe.* **tribes, tribal**

trick |trĭk| *n.* A clever or skillful act: *the dog's new trick.* **tricks, tricked, tricking, tricky, trickier, trickiest, trickster**

trim |trĭm| *v.* To make neat by cutting away unnecessary parts: *to trim the plants.* **trims, trimmed, trimming, trimmer**

trust |trŭst| *n.* A strong belief in someone's honesty, truthfulness, power, etc.: *has your trust.* **trusts, trusted, trusting, trustful, trustless, trustiness**

Tuesday |tōoz′ dā′| *adj.* Of Tuesday: *a Tuesday meeting. n.* The third day of the week: *will mail by Tuesday.* **Tues.**

turtle |tûr′tl| *n.* A reptile whose body is enclosed in a hard round shell: *a turtle in the pond.* **turtles**

twenty |twĕn′tē| *adj.* Two times ten: *twenty minutes ago.* **twenties, twentieth**

twenty-five |twĕn′tē fīv′| *adj.* Five more than twenty: *counted twenty-five times.* **twenty-fives, twenty-fifth**

U

unlock |ŭn lŏk′| *v.* To open the lock of: *hard to unlock.* [see *lock*]

until |ŭn tĭl′| *conj.* Up to the time when: *until it freezes. prep.* Up to the time of: *slept until noon.*

W

wade |wād| *v.* To walk slowly and with difficulty through water, mud, or snow: *to wade across the stream. n.* A slow and difficult walk: *a wade into the ocean.* **wades, waded, wading**

wait |wāt| *v.* To stay in a place until something happens or someone comes: *to wait for the bus.* **waits, waited, waiting, waiter, waitress**

waiting |wā′tĭng| *v.* Staying until something happens or someone comes: *waiting for the rain to stop.* [see *wait*]

ă pat / ā pay / â care / ä father / ĕ pet / ē be / ĭ pit / ī pie / î fierce / ŏ pot / ō go / ô paw, for / oi oil / ŏŏ book /
ōŏ boot / ou out / ŭ cut / û fur / th the / th thin / hw which / zh vision / ə ago, item, pencil, atom, circus
©1977 by Houghton Mifflin Company. Reprinted by permission from THE AMERICAN HERITAGE SCHOOL DICTIONARY.

wake |wāk| *v.* To stop sleeping: *to wake at seven o'clock.* **wakes, waked, woke, waking, waken, wakens, wakened, wakening**

waste |wāst| *n.* Material to be thrown away; garbage: *threw the waste into a bag.* **wastes, wasted, wasting, wasteful, wastefully, waster**

weak |wēk| *adj.* Not having power; faint: *a weak sound.* **weaker, weakest, weakly, weakness**

wear |wâr| *v.* To have on or put on the body: *to wear a coat.* **wears, wore, worn, wearing**

Wednesday |wĕnz´dā´| *n.* The fourth day of the week: *stayed until Wednesday.* **Wed.**

weekend |wēk´ĕnd´| *n.* The time between Friday night and Sunday night: *a weekend away from home.* **weekends**

wheel |wēl| *n.* **1.** Something shaped or used like a wheel: *to steer with the wheel.* **2.** A ring, either solid or with spokes, that turns on its center: *the wheel on the old covered wagon.* **wheels, wheeled, wheeling**

whip |wĭp| *n.* A flexible strap attached to a handle: *snapped the whip. v.* To beat eggs, batter, etc.: *will whip a dozen eggs.* **whips, whipped, whipping**

wind |wīnd| *v.* To wrap or fold around something: *to wind yarn into a ball.* **winds, wound, winding**

wind |wĭnd| *n.* Air that is moving: *knocked down by the wind.* **windy, windier, windiest, winds**

windy |wĭn´dē| *adj.* Having much wind: *a windy day.* [see *wind*]

woke |wōk| *v.* Stopped sleeping: *woke late in the day.* [see *wake*]

woman |wŏŏm´ən| *n.* An adult female human being: *the woman with black hair.* **women, womanly**

women |wĭm´ĭn| *n.* More than one woman: *talking with the women in our town.* [see *woman*]

won't |wōnt| Contraction for *will not: won't finish on time.*

wore |wôr| *v.* Had on or put on the body: *wore a heavy sweater under my jacket.* [see *wear*]

worn |wôrn| *v.* Had on or put on the body: *the shirt you had worn yesterday. adj.* Damaged because of use or wear: *worn, dirty shirt.* [see *wear*]

worry |wûr´ē| *v.* To feel or cause to feel troubled or uneasy: *to worry them by coming home late.* **worries, worried, worrying, worrier**

worth |wûrth| *n.* Value, usefulness, or importance: *gems of great worth.* **worthy, worthless, worthlessness, worthiness**

wound |wound| *adj.* Wrapped or folded around: *wound tightly.* —|wŏŏnd| *n.* An injury or hurt: *a knee wound.* [see *wind*]

wrap |răp| *v.* To cover with paper and tie up: *will wrap the gift.* **wraps, wrapped, wrapping, wrapper**

write |rīt| *v.* **1.** To form words or symbols with a pen, pencil, or other instrument: *to write your name.* **2.** To make up stories, books poems, or articles: *to write for the newspaper.* **writes, wrote, writing, written, writer, writers**

writer |rī´tər| *n.* A person who writes; an author: *a writer of mysteries.* [see *write*]

wrong |rông| *adj.* Not correct: *gave me the wrong answer.* **wrongs, wronged, wronging, wrongly**

Y

yard |yärd| *n.* **1.** An area of ground around a house or other building: *played outside in the yard.* **2.** An area used for a certain kind of business: *a coal yard.* **yards, yardage**

yellow |yĕl´ō| *adj.* Having the color yellow: *a yellow sweater. n.* The color of lemons and gold: *leaves of yellow and red.* **yellows, yellowed, yellowing**

Yellow Pages

Proofreading Tips   178

Spelling Rules   179

Spelling Strategies   181

   Personal Word Lists

   Study Tips

   Approximation

240 Most Useful Words   183

**Homonyms and Other
Troublesome Words**   185

Common Contractions   188

Roots and Affixes   189

   Prefixes

   Suffixes

Proofreading Tips

Finding and correcting the spelling errors in your own writing is an important skill. Try these different ways to check your spelling.

1. Read each word letter by letter, touching every letter with a pencil or pen.

2. Read each word letter by letter, putting a dot under every letter.

3. Have a partner read your work aloud while you check it silently.

4. Read your work out loud to yourself.

5. Read your work backwards, word by word, to yourself.

6. Read through your work. Circle any words that look wrong.

7. Look for words and word parts you often misspell. Double-check their spellings.

8. Check for words that are easy to mix up—*too* instead of *two*, *your* instead of *you're*.

9. Type your work on a computer and use the spell checker. Remember that a spell checker only recognizes that a word is correctly spelled, not that it is correctly used.

10. Find correct spellings wherever you can. Here are some ideas:

    - Try writing the word different ways until it looks right.

    - Say the word slowly. Spell all its syllables.

    - Use what you know about spelling rules, letter sounds, and word shapes.

    - Look for the word on your Personal Spelling List.

    - Have you seen the word somewhere? in a book? on the wall? Find it again.

    - Check the lists in these Yellow Pages.

    - Check a dictionary.

    - Ask someone.

Now make up your own ways to find correct spellings!

Spelling Rules

There are many spelling rules, but only a few of them do most of the work. Nearly all the rules here tell how to add endings to words. *(See pages 190–192 for some of these endings.)* Unlike some spelling "rules," these work most of the time!

FORMING PLURALS ("more than one")

Add *s* to most words:
>   aprons
>   operas
>   exhibits

Add *es* to words ending with *s*, *ss*, *sh*, *ch*, *x*:
>   buses
>   dresses
>   wishes
>   patches
>   boxes

Change the *f* or *fe* at the end of some words to *v* and add *es*:
>   calf, calves
>   wolf, wolves
>   life, lives
>   shelf, shelves
>   self, selves
>   knife, knives

Know the few nouns that change their spellings:
>   child, children
>   foot, feet
>   mouse, mice
>   man, men
>   woman, women
>   tooth, teeth

ADDING ENDINGS BEGINNING WITH A VOWEL TO...

...Words Ending with a Vowel Plus a Consonant

Double the final consonant of a one-syllable word:

> bag, bagged
> grip, gripper
> get, getting
> rot, rotten

Double the final consonant of words with more than one syllable when the last syllable is accented:

> permit, permitted
> regret, regretting

Don't double the final consonant when the last syllable is not accented:

> model, modeling
> travel, traveler

ADDING ENDINGS TO...

...Words Ending with Silent E

Drop the final _e_ when adding an ending that begins with a vowel:

> hurdle, hurdling
> hostile, hostility
> scrape, scraper
> nerve, nervous

Keep the final _e_ when adding an ending that begins with a consonant:

> active, actively
> resource, resourceful
> gentle, gentleness

ADDING ENDINGS TO...

...Words Ending with Y

Add the ending right onto the root when the word ends with a <u>vowel</u> + _y_:

> joy, joyous
> journey, journeyed
> employ, employment
> betray, betraying

Change the _y_ to _i_ before adding the ending when a word ends with a <u>consonant</u> + _y_:

> lady, ladies
> shiny, shiniest
> lucky, luckily
> try, tried

_I_ BEFORE _E_

Remember the rule:
_i_ before _e_, except after _c_, or when rhyming with _say_, as in _neighbor_ and _weigh_:

> believe
> ceiling
> sleigh

but learn the exceptions, too:

> seize
> either
> their
> neither
> weird
> height
> leisure

Spelling Strategies

Perfect spellers are hard to find, but almost anyone can be a good speller. The differences between good spellers and bad spellers are:

> **Good spellers know when words are spelled incorrectly. Bad spellers don't.**

> **Good spellers proofread and correct themselves. Bad spellers don't.**

Following are some strategies for improving your spelling. Try them all. Then think of your own.

PERSONAL WORD LISTS

Make lists—or a personal dictionary—of words you use in your writing. Use them as your own personal references.

1. **Difficult Words.** Collect words that are difficult for you to spell. Write them in alphabetical order so they're easy to find. Study them. Write them. Have a partner test you, and use the Proofreading Tips on page 178 to check your spelling. When you can spell and write a word with ease, cross it out and add a new one. Keep changing your list, and don't let it get too long.

2. **Writing Bank.** The best stories you will write are about what you know. Collect the correct spellings of words that name:

   - family, friends, classmates, people you see and do things with

   - places you go, where they are, what they look like, what you do there, where you live

   - things you do, what interests you, what you wish for, your hobbies, your collections

   - sports, movies, video games you enjoy

   The personal words in your Writing Bank can give you ideas for writing.

3. **Personal Computer File.** If you use a computer, dedicate a file to your personal word lists. Be sure to proofread your word list even if you spell check it. *Sum thymes the spell check excepts a word as write, butt its knot the word yew mien two ewes.*

STUDY TIPS

The list of words you can spell easily gets longer as you study and use words from your regular spelling lists and your daily writing. Here are some ways to learn new words for your list.

1. **S-H-A-R-P.** Use the S-H-A-R-P study procedure on page 3 in your spelling book to study spelling words, difficult words, personal words, or any other words you use in your writing.

2. **Hard Spots.** Pay special attention to parts of a word that give you trouble. Study them extra hard. Be on the lookout for these every time you write.

3. **Memory Tricks.** If all else fails, try a memory trick to remember difficult spellings.

   - Make up a spelling-helper pronunciation: princi**pal**, choc-**o**-late.

   - Use meaning-helper word parts: the **real** in **real**ity; the **ear** in h**ear**.

   - Make up your own memory-helper saying. For example,

     A fri**end** is a fri**end** to the **end**.

     There's one **s** in **s**and in the de**s**ert, and two **s**'s in **s**trawberry **s**hortcake for de**ss**ert.

APPROXIMATION

When you are writing a first draft, you sometimes want to use an exact word, a great word, but you haven't yet learned to spell it. Instead of stopping to make sure you get it right the first time, try this:

1. **Spell the word as best you can.** (This is called "approximation." It means "close, but maybe not quite right.")

2. **Circle the word and continue with your writing.**

3. **After you have finished the first draft, go back and correct the circled word.**

Then add the word to your Personal Word List, study it, and use it the next time you are writing.

240 Most Useful Words

If you can spell these words, more than half of what you write will be correctly spelled. (Words marked * are often misspelled.)

A	B	C	D	E	F	G	H	I
*about	back	called	day	eat	family	game	had	if
after	be	came	did	end	father	gave	happy	I'm
*again	bear	can	*didn't	even	fell	get	has	in
all	*because	car	do	ever	find	girl	have	into
also	bed	cat	dog	*every	fire	give	he	is
*always	*been	*come	*don't		*first	go	head	it
am	*before	*could	door		fish	*going	*heard	*its
an	best		down		five	gone	help	*it's
and	big				food	good	her	
another	black				for	got	here	
any	book				form		him	
are	boy				found		his	
around	brother				*four		home	
as	but				*friend		horse	
asked	*by				fun		*house	
at							how	
away								

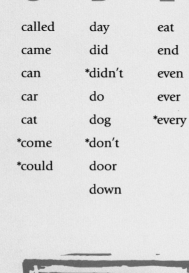

J

just

K

*knew
*know

L

land
last
left
like
*little
live
long
look
*lot
love

M

mad
made
man
*many
may
me
men
money
more
*morning
most
*mother
much
my

N

name
need
never
new
next
nice
*night
no
not
now

O

of
*off
oh
old
on
*once
one
only
or
other
our
out
over

P

*people
place
*play
put

R

ran
*really
red
ride
*right
room
run

S

*said
saw
say
school
see
she
should
sister
small
so
*some
*something
*sometimes
*soon
spring
started
still
*summer
*swimming

T

take
tell
ten
*than
that
the
*their
them
*then
*there
these
*they
thing
think
this
three
*through
time
to
told
*too
took
tree
tried
two

V

*very

W

walk
want
wanted
was
water
way
we
well
went
*were
what
*when
*where
*which
while
*white
who
why
will
with
woods
work
*would

Y

year
yes
you
*your

words

Homonyms and Other Troublesome Words

Some words sound alike but have different spellings and meanings. They are easy to confuse when you write.

accept, except
Please **accept** my invitation.

Everyone was invited **except** me.

allowed, aloud
Smoking is not **allowed**.

The teacher reads **aloud** to the class.

a lot (2 words)
I have **a lot** of homework today.

already, all ready
He's **already** finished.

Now he's **all ready** to leave.

ant, aunt
An **ant** was on my sandwich.

My **aunt** and uncle are here!

ate, eight
Who **ate** the last piece?

We hiked for nearly **eight** hours.

been, bin
Where have you **been**?

She stored the vegetables in a **bin**.

blew, blue
Everyone **blew** whistles at the same time.

I'm black and **blue** from the scrimmage.

by, buy
Come **by** when you're finished.

You can **buy** whatever you want.

capital, capitol
Begin each sentence with a **capital**.

The state **capitol** is a beautiful building.

cent, sent, scent
It didn't cost a **cent**.

Someone **sent** it to her.

The perfume has the **scent** of roses.

chews, choose
He **chews** each bite slowly.

Let's **choose** up teams!

close, clothes
Did you remember to **close** the door?

I have to hang up my **clothes**.

do, dew, due
Do you remember what you did?

The grass was still wet with morning **dew**.

When is our science report **due**?

for, four

> I'll buy something **for** you.
>
> I need **four** pencils for school.

hear, here

> Did you **hear** a scraping sound?
>
> We're the only ones **here**.

heard, herd

> He **heard** the soft lowing of the cattle.
>
> The **herd** was a bit restless.

hole, whole

> Put the round peg in the round **hole**.
>
> You have to finish the **whole** puzzle.

hour, our

> It'll take at least an **hour**.
>
> We'll do **our** best.

its, it's

> The ball has lost **its** bounce.
>
> Maybe **it's** time to get another one.

know, no

> Does he **know** her?
>
> I have **no** idea.

knows, nose

> Nobody **knows** the way.
>
> His sensitive **nose** will find the way.

lay, lie

> **Lay** the boxes on the floor.
>
> Now go and **lie** down for a while.

lets, let's

> Everyone **lets** him do what he wants.
>
> **Let's** wait and see what happens.

new, knew

> Is that a **new** shirt you're wearing?
>
> I **knew**, because it was so smooth.

not, knot

> We're **not** going to be able to go yet.
>
> Can you untie this **knot**?

past, passed

> It's half **past** nine and I'm finished.
>
> We **passed** the slow-moving truck.

peace, piece

> Everyone prefers **peace** to war.
>
> My favorite **piece** is the crusty corner.

plain, plane

> He wore a **plain** green sweater.
>
> The **plane** prepared for takeoff.

presents, presence

> The **presents** were wrapped in white paper.
>
> Her **presence** in the room quieted the class.

principle, principal

> He is a person of high **principles**.
>
> "The **principal** is your pal" is a mnemonic device.

quit, quite, quiet

I wish he'd **quit** talking.

I'm not **quite** ready to go yet.

The baby's sleeping so try to be **quiet**.

right, write

Do we turn left, or **right**?

Why don't you **write** yourself a letter?

some, sum

Don't you have **some** homework?

The **sum** of 3456 + 6543 is 9999.

stationary, stationery

The fort was a **stationary** target.

The letter was written on pink **stationery**.

than, then

No one can run faster **than** you!

She sang one song, **then** she sang another.

there, their, they're

Put it over **there** by the sink.

Are the campers in **their** cabins?

They said **they're** going to help us.

theirs, there's

Are these jackets **theirs** or yours?

Where **there's** smoke, **there's** fire.

through, threw

She walked **through** the gate.

You **threw** away a perfectly good boot!

to, too, two

Go **to** jail.

Go there directly, **too**.

Do not collect **two** hundred dollars.

way, weigh

Show me the **way** to go home.

That must **weigh** a ton!

weak, week

I'm not as **weak** as I look.

In a **week**, they're going on vacation.

wear, where

What are you going to **wear**?

If I knew **where** we're going, I'd tell you.

weather, whether

We're having mild **weather**.

We'll go **whether** it rains or not.

which, witch

I don't know **which** book to read first.

Is she the good **witch** or the bad one?

who's, whose

Who's ready for dessert?

Do you know **whose** hat is on the chair?

wood, would

The ship model is carved from **wood**.

He said he **would** probably sell it.

your, you're

Is this **your** book?

Thanks, **you're** a good friend to return it.

Common Contractions

A contraction is a word made by joining two words. An apostrophe is used to take the place of the letter(s) left out.

   is + not = isn't   it + is = it's

Contractions are **not** difficult to spell once you understand the way they are formed.

VERB + *not*

is . . . . isn't
are . . . . aren't
was . . . . wasn't
were . . . . weren't
have . . . . haven't
has . . . . hasn't
had . . . . hadn't
do . . . . don't
does . . . . doesn't
did . . . . didn't
can . . . . can't
could . . . . couldn't
must . . . . mustn't
will . . . . won't
would . . . . wouldn't
should . . . . shouldn't

PRONOUN + VERB

		am	I'm
		will	I'll
I	+	have	= I've
		had	I'd
		would	I'd
		are	you're, we're, they're
you		will	you'll, we'll, they'll
we	+	have	= you've, we've, they've
they		had	you'd, we'd, they'd
		would	you'd, we'd, they'd
		is	he's, she's, it's
he		will	he'll, she'll, it'll
she	+	has	= he's, she's, it's
it		had	he'd, she'd, it'd
		would	he'd, she'd, it'd

OTHER CONTRACTIONS

In talk, informal writing, and written dialog, contracted words are common. Each word in column 1, for example, can form a contraction with most words in column 2.

1		2		
who		is		_____'s
what		are		_____'re
when		will		_____'ll
where	+	has	=	_____'s
why		have		_____'ve
here		had		_____'d
there		would		_____'d

Roots and Affixes

A root is a word or word part without additions.
You can often add affixes to roots to make new words.
A prefix is an affix at the beginning of a word.
A suffix is an affix at the end of a word.

danger	root word
en**danger**	prefix + **root**
dangerous	**root** + suffix
en**danger**ed	prefix + **root** + suffix
unen**danger**ed	prefix + prefix + **root** + suffix
dangerously	**root** + suffix + suffix

If you know how to spell the root, how to spell common affixes, and the spelling rules for adding suffixes (See pages 179–180), you know how to spell thousands and thousands of words.

Here are some of the extra words you can spell just by adding prefixes and suffixes to the words **person** and **simple**. Notice that adding a suffix sometimes changes the spelling of the root word.

personify	**person**able	**simpl**er	**simpl**ification
personal	**person**age	**simpl**est	un**simpl**ifed
im**person**al	**person**alize	**simpl**y	over**simpl**ification
inter**person**al	de**person**alize	**simpl**ify	**simpl**eton
personality	im**person**ation	**simpl**icity	

The Other Word Forms in your spelling lessons and the following lists will help you multiply the number of words you know how to spell.

PREFIXES

Many of your spelling words are root words that can become new words
with new meanings when a prefix is added. Adding a prefix does not usually
change the spelling of the root word. In addition, many English words are made
of prefixes combined with ancient Greek and Latin root words.

	Prefix	Meaning	Examples
how much,	semi-	half, twice	semifinal, semicircle
how many	tri-	three	triangle, tricycle
	kilo-	thousand	kilogram, kilometer
	micro-	very small	microscopic, microfilm
	dec-	ten	decade, decimal
	mono-	one, single	monorail, monologue
	multi-	much, many	multimillionaire, multipurpose
	bi-	two	bicycle, bilingual
where	sub-	under, below	submarine, submerge
	geo-	earth, of the earth	geography, geologist
	by-	near	bypass, bystander
	circum-	round	circumpolar, circumscribe
	in-	into	inhale, inflate
	inter-	between	interrupt, intercom
	trans-	across, elsewhere	transatlantic, transplant
	under-	below	underpass, underground
	tele-	distant	telephone, telescope
	de-	from	decaf, detour
	mid-	middle	midsummer, midday
	en-	cause to be, in	endangered, enclose
	off-	from	off-line, offshore
	extra-	outside	extraterrestrial, extraordinary
	on-	on	onlooker, onshore
not	im-	not	impatient, immobile
	anti-	opposite of, against	antifreeze, antisocial
	ir-	opposite, not	irresponsible, irresistible
	non-	opposite of, not	nonstop, nonfiction
when	pre-	before	preheat, prefix
	fore-	before, in front of	forefather, forecast
	post-	later, after (in time)	postscript, postwar
	pro-	forward	proceed, progress

extent	super-	over, above, greater	superhighway, superhuman
	over-	too much	overcrowd, overcome
	out-	more	outran, outnumber
who	co-	together	co-author, copilot
	auto-	self, by itself	autograph, autobiography
	self-	self	self-respect, self-taught

SUFFIXES

You can make many new words by adding suffixes to the ends of root words.
The Other Word Forms of your spelling lessons show the many new words
you can spell simply by adding a few endings to the spelling words.

Remember that the spelling of the root word may change when you add a
suffix: **marry/marri**age, **excel/excell**ent, **nerve/nerv**ous. (See the Spelling Rules
on page 180.)

Suffix	Meaning	Examples
-able	able to be	enjoyable, favorable, comfortable, acceptable
-ade	action of	blockade, escapade, barricade, promenade
-age	action of	postage, marriage, package, pilgrimage
-al	relating to	natural, musical, maternal, trial
-ance	state of	allegiance, annoyance, repentance, resistance
-ation	state of	starvation, fascination, inspiration, admiration
-ence	state of being	confidence, dependence, difference, absence
-ent	being or condition	excellent, confident, president, provident
-er	one who, more	teacher, printer, buyer; smaller, larger, faster
-ese	language, native of	Japanese, Chinese, Vietnamese, Portuguese
-hood	state of	childhood, adulthood, falsehood, statehood
-ian	relating to	barbarian, librarian, Houstonian, physician
-ible	causing, able to be	contemptible, terrible, gullible, eligible
-ic	relating to	aquatic, comic, public, historic, lunatic
-ify	to make	simplify, clarify, beautify, mummify, purify
-ing	material that	bedding, frosting, roofing, stuffing, lining
-ion	state of	admission, action, suspicion, companion
-ism	action or condition	enthusiasm, patriotism, baptism, heroism
-ist	one who	dentist, geologist, physicist, aerialist, cyclist
-ity	state of	ability, activity, electricity, locality, vanity
-ive	tending to	adhesive, active, evasive, captive, creative
-ize	to make or do	monopolize, specialize, vaporize, magnetize
-less	without	needless, careless, useless, regardless

-logy	subject of study	mineralogy, biology, phrenology, astrology
-ly	quality of	motherly, hourly, boldly, patiently, dryly
-ment	quality of	agreement, amusement, argument, amazement
-ness	state of	kindness, happiness, quickness, firmness
-or	action or work	governor, inventor, escalator, doctor, actor
-ous	nature of	mountainous, envious, ambitious, generous
-ship	state of	friendship, statesmanship, hardship, ownership
-some	action or state	awesome, tiresome, quarrelsome, burdensome
-teen	number 10	thirteen, fifteen, seventeen, nineteen
-th	number	fourth, tenth, hundredth, thousandth, millionth
-ty	state or condition	priority, loyalty, honesty, unity, conformity
-ure	action	failure, censure, exposure, enclosure, signature

CREDITS
Cover Design: Design Five
Photography: Joseph Sachs
Text Illustrations:
Maxie Chambliss
    pages 29, 43, 59, 101, 102, 125
Ruth Flanigan
    pages 17, 94, 95, 134
Shana Greger
    pages 49, 114
Jennifer Hewitson
    pages 24, 25, 142, 143
Judy Love
    pages 10, 62, 90
Claude Martinot
    pages 109, 110
Jennifer D. Paley
    pages 18, 19, 34, 83
Lauren Scheuer
    pages 38, 55, 105, 130
Brad Teare
    pages 7, 81, 106, 126